# In the Shadow of Russia

**Eurasian Political Economy and Public Policy Studies Series**

# In the Shadow of Russia

## Reform in Kazakhstan and Uzbekistan

Pamela Blackmon

Michigan State University Press • East Lansing

♾ The paper used in this publication meets the minimum requirements of ANSI/NISO
Z39.48-1992 (R 1997) (Permanence of Paper).

Michigan State University Press
East Lansing, Michigan 48823-5245
www.msupress.msu.edu

Printed and bound in the United States of America.

17  16  15  14  13  12  11     1  2  3  4  5  6  7  8  9  10

LIBRARY OF CONGRESS CATALOGING-IN-PUBLICATION DATA
Blackmon, Pamela.
In the shadow of Russia : reform in Kazakhstan and Uzbekistan / Pamela Blackmon.
p. cm. (Eurasian political economy and public policy studies series)
Includes bibliographical references and index.
ISBN 978-0-87013-986-4 (pbk. : alk. paper)
1. Kazakhstan—Economic policy—1991- 2. Uzbekistan—Economic policy—1991- I. Title.
HC420.5.B55 2010
338.95845—dc22
2010021396

Cover design by Erin Kirk New
Book design by Charlie Sharp, Sharp Designs, Lansing, MI

g green    Michigan State University Press is a member of the Green Press Initiative
  press    and is committed to developing and encouraging ecologically responsible
  INITIATIVE
publishing practices. For more information about the Green Press Initiative and the use of
recycled paper in book publishing, please visit *www.greenpressinitiative.com*.

Visit Michigan State University Press on the World Wide Web at *www.msupress.msu.edu*.

# Contents

vii      Figures and Tables

ix      Acknowledgments

1      Introduction

15    1    Breaking Apart from Russia

29    2    Agreeing to Manage Economic Policies in Uzbekistan

47    3    Economics Determines Politics for Nazarbayev

67    4    Connecting Specific Reform Policies to Investment and Business

93      Conclusion

101      Notes

115      References

127      Index

# Figures and Tables

## Figures

16    **1**    Kazakhstan's Electricity Production, 1991–2000

17    **2**    Kazakhstan's Exports of Coking Coal to the Baltics, Russia, and Other FSU States, 1993–2000

19    **3**    Uzbekistan's Natural Gas Balance, 1991–2000

20    **4**    Uzbekistan's Production and Consumption of Natural Gas, 1999–2007

## Tables

22    **1**    Production of Raw Cotton in the Seven Highest Producing Oblasts in Uzbekistan, 1960–1970

33    **2**    Uzbek State Officials, Pre- and Post-Soviet Periods

37    **3**    Uzbekistan's Balance of Payments, 1995–1997

39    **4**    Important Uzbek Officials and Positions in the Government, 1992–2005

43    **5**    EBRD Rating of Trade and Foreign Exchange System and Benchmarks of Reform for Uzbekistan, 1991–2008

44    **6**    EBRD Rating of Trade and Foreign Exchange System and Benchmarks of Reform for Kazakhstan, 1991–2008

52    **7**    Kazakh State Officials, November 1992

60    **8**    Significant Legislation Decreed after the Disbanding of the March 1995 Parliament

68    **9**    Net FDI Inflows in the Former Soviet Union Successor States

69    **10**    Cumulative FDI Inflows in the Former Soviet Union Successor States and Natural Resource Endowment Ranking

74    **11**    Standard Industrial Classifications (*sic*) of Surveyed Firms

75    **12**    Results of Questionnaire, Natural Resource Firms

84    **13**    Results of Questionnaire, Business Firms

89    **14**    EBRD Rating of Banking Reform and Interest Rate Liberalization for Kazakhstan and Uzbekistan, 1991–2008

91    **15**    Firms' Perceptions of Economic Reform and Risk

# Acknowledgments

have many persons to thank for their assistance with this book. First, I am very grateful to Roger Kanet for his consistent advice and support from the very beginning of this project. Roger has been a great mentor and source of advice for me as I have moved through academia. It has been an honor to have such a well-respected scholar involved with my research. I would also like to thank Richard Weisskoff for making the initial introductions to some of the economists working at the International Monetary Fund, many of whom I subsequently interviewed. Darrell Slider, Jan Nijman, Clair Apodaca, Joel Jenswold, and Mark White all provided important feedback and comments on various drafts and at different stages of the project. I would especially like to thank Norm Graham, Folke Lindahl, the anonymous reviewers of Michigan State University Press, and Julie Loehr and the other editors at the press for their very insightful and supportive comments as this manuscript progressed into a book.

I would like to acknowledge the financial and institutional support that I received for this project. The pilot study award from the Department of International Studies at the University of Miami allowed me to travel to Washington, D.C., to conduct interviews numerous times at the International Monetary Fund and the World Bank, as well as to buy publications for my research. I was also selected as a visiting scholar in residence at the American Political Science Association's Centennial Center, located in Washington, D.C. My stay there allowed me to conduct follow-up interviews with economists at the IMF and the World Bank, with persons in the business community, and with numerous other experts in

Washington, D.C. These interviews comprised a substantial part of the research for this book. I am very grateful for all of the individuals that were kind enough to agree to be interviewed. While they will remain anonymous, they took time out of their busy schedules to talk to me and answer my questions. This book would not have been as strong without their expertise and advice. My stay at the Centennial Center was a memorable one, and I would like to thank Michael Britnall, Robert Hauck, Sean Twombly, and the other staff at the Centennial Center for their advice and support. In addition, the other scholars in residence, Katrina Gamble, Dorian Woods, Michael Heaney, and Kevin Quigley comprised an important group for advice and support. I also thank Taylor and Francis Ltd for permission to reprint some material from "Back to the USSR: Why the Past Does Matter in Explaining Differences in the Economic Reform Processes of Kazakhstan and Uzbekistan" and "Divergent Paths, Divergent Outcomes: Linking Differences in Economic Reform to Levels of US Direct Foreign Investment and Business in Kazakhstan and Uzbekistan."

Many family members also provided words of encouragement and support during the research and writing. My parents, Bill and Betty Lyle, and my in-laws, Judy and Marty Freedman, were great sources of encouragement, as were their greater circles of family and friends. My son Benjamin has been a fun and wonderful addition to our family and often served as the inspiration that I needed to keep writing. However, I owe the most gratitude to my husband, Jason Freedman. It is not an understatement to say that I could not have completed this book without his constant support and encouragement. I feel very fortunate to have him in my life.

# Introduction

I t has now been two decades since the dissolution of the Soviet Union and the emergence from it of fifteen independent republics. These new states embarked on unprecedented transitions from economies in which the government made all economic decisions into market-oriented economies. Indeed, many of these new states had never functioned with any type of a market structure, nor even existed as political units within their current boundaries. In these unprecedented circumstances, the newly independent republics followed various paths toward market economies. The purpose of this book is to explain the divergent economic reform processes of two of these former Soviet republics: Kazakhstan and Uzbekistan.

Kazakhstan and Uzbekistan, the two largest of the five Central Asian republics by land area and population respectively, began their economic reform almost in tandem. In 1992, both countries initiated programs to privatize state-owned assets and to liberalize controls in order to allow the market, instead of the government, to set prices for goods. A problem with price liberalization was the likelihood of inflation, as prices of goods formerly controlled were allowed to reach levels determined by the market. Therefore, the transition economies were advised by the IMF and other economic advisors to establish stabilization programs to control inflation. Kazakhstan enacted its stabilization program in January 1994; Uzbekistan followed in November 1994. At this point their progress toward reform diverged, with Kazakhstan proceeding further in that direction, and Uzbekistan slowing almost to a halt. Thus the question: Why did Kazakhstan continue its economic reforms, while Uzbekistan did not?

Kazakhstan had completed price liberalization by the end of 1994, effectively ending the role of the government in setting prices. Uzbekistan liberalized most prices by the end of 1996, but the government continued to set energy prices and kept the state order system for goods produced domestically, such as cotton and grain (IMF 1995, 13). The countries diverged most markedly in their reform policies in 1996. In that year, Kazakhstan agreed to allow its currency to be completely convertible, meaning that the government would no longer attempt to control its reserves of foreign currency. This single decision was one of the most important economic reforms that the county had implemented to date.[1] In that same year, Kazakhstan was also able to secure an advanced loan through the International Monetary Fund that allowed the country to focus on additional areas of structural reform. Uzbekistan, on the other hand, implemented an institutionalized multiple exchange rate regime in 1996 in order to improve its balance of payments and to maintain control over currency reserves. As a result of the decision to continue this distorted exchange rate system, the IMF suspended its only lending arrangement with Uzbekistan in March 1997. Uzbekistan did not until 2003 agree to allow its currency to be convertible. This volume will explain why Kazakhstan continued with economic reform and lessened governmental involvement in the economy, whereas Uzbekistan stopped reform policies and increased governmental involvement in the economy.

Relatively early in the transition process, observers began to categorize the former Soviet republics in two groups: the advanced reformers and the later reformers. The countries in Central and Eastern Europe (CEE) and the Baltic states became known as advanced reformers because they had made the most progress in first political and then economic reforms. Political reforms included the change from Communist to democratic governments. The different choices that the former Communist states made about their new political and economic systems were influenced by a number of factors. The CEE and the Baltic states had longer legacies of democratic government and a market economy than the former Soviet republics and wanted to implement policies that would get them closer to membership in the European Union (Orenstein 2001; Orenstein and Haas 2005, 136). In addition to the influence of their pre-Soviet history, the geographical proximity to Western Europe (and Western markets) was an additional reason the CEE and Baltic states proceeded with reform more quickly than the former Soviet Union countries.[2] A logical conclusion to draw from the experience of these advanced reformers was that the political reform coupled with the economic reform had led to their early success. The early comparative statistical analyses of the transition economies carried out by Anders Åslund, Peter Boone, and Simon Johnson (1996) and Steven Fish (1998) confirmed that a change in political leadership (non-Communist) led to progress in economic reforms.

The former Soviet republics were categorized as the later reformers because they made less progress than did the CEE and Baltic states in reform. However, the divergent reform processes of Kazakhstan and Uzbekistan present a puzzle because neither country has created a non-Communist democratic government. Nursultan Nazarbayev and Islam Karimov became head of the Communist Party of their respective republic in 1989 and were elected to the position of president in December 1991. Each man has served as president ever since. Presidential elections were held in Kazakhstan in December 2005, and while Nazarbayev won with wide margins, the elections were not considered free and fair by international standards. Karimov won Uzbekistan's presidential elections held in December 2007; however, they were even less democratic, and international observers did not even bother to send a full delegation to observe them. So while both countries can generally be categorized as authoritarian, Kazakhstan has been termed "mildly authoritarian," while Uzbekistan has been described as a "full-fledged authoritarian" regime (Åslund 2007, 214).

Therefore, other factors must explain the variation in the reform efforts of these two countries. Indeed, both geographic proximity to Europe and the influence of the pre-Soviet era in the CEE and Baltic states are important factors affecting those countries' processes of reform. This study builds upon conceptual frameworks that include geography and choices about economic integration in an analysis of the reforms of Kazakhstan and Uzbekistan. My argument is that post-Soviet developments in these states have been greatly influenced by the Soviet past. Specifically, I argue that differences in the reform policies in these two states have been shaped by geographic, political, and economic structures in place during the Soviet era. The following central questions are addressed: How and in what areas did a republic's level of integration with Soviet-era Russia influence its present economic orientation? What are the contributing factors that explain differences between leaders (of a similar regime type) in their decisions about economic reform? In order to answer these questions, I use information from both the economic and the political literature on post-Communist transitions, undertaking a comprehensive analysis of the reform processes of Kazakhstan and Uzbekistan.

## The Post-Communist Transition

The end of the Soviet Union and the subsequent emergence of fifteen independent republics resulted in unprecedented challenges for the fields of economics and political science. Primarily, this was because these new states were not simply heavily distorted market economies that required structural assistance from the institutions of the IMF and the World Bank (as were, for example, Latin American countries such as Argentina and Brazil during the 1980s).[3] Instead, except for the CEE and Baltic states, the former Soviet economies had functioned without any traditional market structure (Winiecki 1995; World Bank 1996). One of the more pressing concerns during the post-Communist transition was decreasing the role of the state in decision making and thereby ending the power of the state bureaucracy and the power of the elite. Reformers believed that the most efficient way to accomplish this shift in power was through democracy, the results of which would eliminate leaders who had vested interests in opposing economic reform. Anders Åslund (2007, 36) makes the point succinctly: "It was vital for the substance of democracy to disarm the old elite through radical reform."

The early economic reform strategy that the former socialist economies were advised to follow centered on shock therapy, or the "big bang" approach, because it involved implementing macroeconomic reforms and structural adjustment policies simultaneously. Economists such as Stanley Fischer and Jacob Frenkel (1992) recommended that post-Soviet countries undertake, as soon as possible, macroeconomic stabilization, the liberalization of the prices of most goods, current account convertibility of the currency, the creation of a social safety net, and privatization. David Lipton and Jeffrey Sachs (1990, 99) argued that the transition process needed to be both rapid and comprehensive because elements of the process were necessarily tied together. They justified this approach by explaining that "structural reforms cannot work without a working price system; a working price system cannot be put in place without ending excess demand and creating a convertible currency." Åslund (1989; 1992; 1995) concurred with prescription for shock therapy, and his justifications included references to the structure of the Soviet political and economic system. This was important because many of these early economic reform strategies did not adequately recognize how the different experiences of the republics during the Soviet past would influence their policies as independent states. For example, Åslund (2002, 80) explained that the full liberalization of prices was necessary because "partial liberalization . . . facilitated arbitrage by the privileged between regulated prices and free prices." A slower or gradual pace of reform was a concern because it could lead to rent-seeking among the elite, a way for them to benefit from the incomplete liberalization of prices. Radical reforms were necessary to completely change the system to a market economy; there was concern that if the reforms were not comprehensive enough, they would not work and there would be popular support to reverse them (Gomułka 1989; Kornai 1990; Balcerowicz 1995). Again, the need for radical and comprehensive reforms provided the justification for the focus on political reform, a change to non-Communist and (theoretically) democratic political leadership.

There were proponents of more gradual reform programs, but these scholars did not focus on how Soviet-era circumstances would affect differences in the approaches of the former Communist countries. The gradualists, as they were called, were primarily concerned that economic reforms were too rapid and that adequate social policies and an appropriate legal framework were not in place to protect citizens. Joseph Stiglitz (2002) and others (Amsden, Kochanowicz, and Taylor 1994; Nolan 1995) argued that the Chinese model of limited governmental control (or gradual privatization) over some sectors of industry until they could adjust to market policies was more advisable than complete privatization. The gradualists also believed that economic reforms were taking precedence over social policies that would be needed to protect citizens from the shocks and inequities of a new economic system. Indeed, ten years after the end of the Soviet Union a World Bank study found that in Eastern Europe and Central Asia the segment of the population living on less than one dollar a day had increased from 1.5 percent in 1990 to 5.1 percent in 1998 (World Bank 2002, 8). Since under the Soviet system the state had provided social services, including a social safety net for its citizens, gradualists believed that the economic transformation required a greater focus on adequate social policies. Another concern of the gradualists was that not enough attention was paid to the establishment of a legal framework during the transition. Peter Murrell (Murrell 1992; Murrell and Wang 1993; Murell et al. 1997) wrote extensively about this problem, pointing out that a legal framework would be necessary for privatization of formerly state owned property. Murrell (2001, 3) later lamented that "as a succession of shock therapies and big bangs were announced, legal and institutional reforms receded into the background." Even Åslund (2007, 245) subsequently admitted that "the construction of an effective legal system should be one of the foremost tasks of postcommunist transition."

The proponents of these different early economic reform strategies disagreed about the sequencing and the pace at which economic, political, and social reforms should be implemented in the transition economies. In fact, many of these theorists still do not agree about whether shock therapy was the best strategy or whether countries that implemented more gradual reforms performed better. Stiglitz (2007, 54) still defends the gradualist approach, asserting starkly, "Shock therapy failed in Russia." Åslund (2007, 308) on the other hand, defends shock therapy: "A market economy could be built, and the radical market reform program worked."[4] Theorists of both schools of thought can point to examples in various countries that suggest their particular policy choices were the correct ones. Mitchell Orenstein's (2001) conclusions about the transition strategies in Poland and the Czech Republic provide support for the use of both types of policy, depending on the economic and political circumstances. He finds that governments in various countries responded to different political and economic circumstances and used both strategies successfully in their transitions.

In hindsight, as Orenstein illustrates, there are merits to both approaches. The benefits of shock therapy include the fact that the painful reforms have for the most part been implemented. Uzbekistan, by contrast, will struggle because the country did not continue to implement macroeconomic reforms. However, all of the post-Communist countries have struggled to improve their socioeconomic indicators, even the ones that pursued more gradualist privatization, such as Poland (Orenstein 2001, 9; Stiglitz 2007, 39).

Unfortunately, neither of the two perspectives I have described adequately incorporated the effect of the republics' different experiences during the Soviet era past, which would likely influence their decisions as independent states. In other words, not enough attention was paid to the factors that would influence their choices on economic policy. While recommending particular strategies of reform is important, it is equally important to understand what limitations might impede their implementation.

Rawi Abdelal (2001) and Andrei Tsygankov (2001) found, for example, that nationalism and national identity were strong factors in determining the policies of post-Soviet states and that those identities were formed before the end of the Soviet Union. Indeed, more contemporary research on these countries has incorporated analysis of the degree to which circumstances during the Soviet era have influenced the present economic situation in the post-Soviet states (Blackmon 2005; 2009; Rumer 2005; Pomfret 2006). This book will examine three factors that greatly influenced decisions about economic reform in these states: the level of integration with Soviet-era Russia; the relationships between the leaders and the elite; and the degree to which economic reform affects levels of investment and business. The following sections describe each of these factors and how they contribute to an explanation of the divergent reform processes in Kazakhstan and Uzbekistan.

## Geography and Physical Infrastructure

Many assumptions about the political organization of the Central Asian states after the end of the Soviet Union have proven incorrect. These countries did not pursue pre-Soviet identities along tribal or religious (Islamic) divisions (Jones Luong 2004, 12). Nor did any Central Asian state, apart from Tajikistan, experience a violent civil war. Finally, as Pauline Jones Luong comments, "post-Soviet Central Asian leaders have not wholly rejected, but rather strategically incorporated, the Soviet institutional and policy legacies of which they were an integral part" (2004, 12). Indeed, according to Jones Luong (2002), the recently formed states forged new identities based in part on their Soviet history. This book will provide evidence to indicate that the development of these new identities was shaped by the degree of each republic's integration with Soviet-era Russia.

Kazakhstan borders Russia to its north, and because of its natural resources and other factors, Kazakhstan was more economically integrated than other republics with Soviet-era Russia in a number of key areas of infrastructure. In fact, Kazakhstan's electrical power, industrial production, and oil and gas pipeline structures were all linked with Russia's during the Soviet era. This interwoven relationship constrained the country's capacity to operate as a closed and independent economy. For example, beginning with its independence, Kazakhstan registered decreases in electrical production due to interruptions from the grids on the Russian side mainly, as the Kazakh grids were part of a larger system; they were never designed to function independently from Russia's. Therefore, Kazakhstan had to develop entirely new electrical structures and enterprises to manage these systems and chose to privatize large portions of its electrical power sectors in order to attract foreign investors (see World Bank 1999, 4–9). In addition, even though the country has sizable reserves of oil, it did not have its own dedicated pipeline routes for the export of oil, and under the Soviet system Kazakhstan's oil was exported solely to Russia. This market exclusivity prompted the country to implement foreign investment and tax legislation in the mid-1990s to attract investment for its oil and gas sectors. Thus, I attribute Kazakhstan's decision to agree to currency convertibility, to move ahead with its privatization program, and to implement legislation to encourage investment as steps in part designed to disengage itself from Russia.

Uzbekistan has its own story and is more distant from Russia, bordering Afghanistan to the south. Uzbekistan is also endowed with natural resources, although the types of resources and, thus, the republic's structural connections to Soviet-era Russia were different. Uzbekistan was a substantial producer of primary products such as cotton, gold, and natural gas during the Soviet era, and all but the latter were exported to Moscow. At independence, the country was the fourth largest producer of cotton and the eighth largest producer of gold in the world. Uzbekistan's favorable terms of trade—its ability to export its resources of cotton and gold and to keep its industry functioning through its natural gas reserves—allowed the republic to perform at relatively the same economic level at independence. Uzbekistan's greater distance from Russia meant that the two countries did not operate at the same level of integration as Kazakhstan with Russia did during the Soviet era, and so the Uzbek government was able to follow a more gradual approach to economic reform.

## Determining Supporters and Opponents of Reform

This study focuses on the actions of the leaders in decisions regarding economic reform, and related to this, decisions made about the continuation of the former Soviet elite in the government after independence. Sally Cummings's study of the political elite in Kazakhstan explains that even though determining its makeup is difficult, it is crucial to focus "on the first dimension of power, i.e. who matters in the decision-making process" (2005, 10). My analysis of persons in key governmental positions in Kazakhstan and Uzbekistan relied on two methodological strategies to identify the elite: positional and decisional analysis.[5]

The positional approach begins from the premise that powerful people hold positions in government and that they derive their power from these institutional roles. This is one of the most common research techniques since formal institutions keep records on personnel. Records were rather meticulously kept during the Soviet era, although not all in one coherent place, so information is derived from both primary and secondary sources. I employ decisional analysis because it focuses on the way in which important decisions were made and by which important actors. The benefits of this approach are explained by Cummings (2005, 11): "This method [decisional analysis]—sometimes called event analysis—is based on the assumption that, if political power is defined in terms of influence over government activities, we can detect it by studying the means by which specific decisions are reached and, in particular, by identifying the individuals who successfully initiate or veto proposals."

My analysis of persons in key governmental positions in Uzbekistan and Kazakhstan combines these approaches in the following ways. First, persons in more than one position were identified as having the trust of the president, and therefore judged important. Second, I followed the career of these persons in subsequent years to determine if they continued in the government, either in the same position or in a different one. Finally, I attempted to determine if the officials had held positions in the government of either of the two republics during the Soviet era. In Uzbekistan, Karimov appointed trusted persons to governmental positions throughout 1992–2005, many of whom served in the Uzbek government during the Soviet era. In Kazakhstan, Nazarbayev also appointed trusted persons to serve in governmental positions, but none of them continued past 1993, and none had served in the Kazakh government during the Soviet era.

The leaders of Kazakhstan and Uzbekistan have differed markedly in their decisions on the implementation of reform. Joel Hellman (1998) has contributed to the examination of the leaders' role in economic policy by formulating a theory on why leaders would implement partial economic reform. He argues that opponents of post-Communist reform were the net winners early in the reform process and did not want to give up their gains. Therefore, these "short-term winners have often sought to stall the economy in a partial reform equilibrium that generates concentrated rents for themselves, while imposing high costs on the rest of society" (Hellman 1998, 204–5). Gerald Easter has examined Uzbekistan's post-Communist transition and finds that "presidentialism [over parliamentarism] was preferred by those old regime elites who in the process of regime breakdown maintained their access, completely or partially, to the state's power resources" (1997, 189). My analysis contributes to an understanding of the decisions about reform efforts and groups that benefited from those efforts in Kazakhstan and Uzbekistan.

In Uzbekistan, Karimov's support comes from people who benefit from economic distortions, primarily the Uzbek leadership remaining from the Soviet-era elite. This political framework has shaped much of the postindependence development of Uzbekistan, which focused on a continuation of distorted political and economic policies that benefited Soviet-era holdovers among the elite. Martha Brill Olcott argues that Uzbekistan's further delay in implementing economic reform during 2001–3 was due in part to a desire by the elite to "keep the economic playing field frozen in place to maximize their own potential for patronage and personal wealth" (2005, 119–20).

In Kazakhstan, on the other hand, Nazarbayev's support is derived from groups benefiting from economic reforms, including a new elite class that took advantage of the privatization of formerly state-owned assets.[6] Jonathan Murphy's analysis of the transformation in Kazakhstan finds support for a "durable power elite" that was able to move up in employment and state positions based, in part, on its allegiance to the Nazarbayev government and its policies.[7] Murphy's findings, as well as those of this book, are in sharp contrast to the dominant perspective, which is that the elite in Kazakhstan grew out of clan-based affiliations. According to this clan-based perspective, the elite in post-Soviet countries can be identified based on clan membership (see, e.g., Collins 2002, 142; 2004a; Schatz 2004). Clan-based affiliations (which focus on the influence of the pre-Soviet era) may explain some membership of the elite, but the evidence indicates the relationship between the elite and the president is based on support or opposition to the president's economic policies. In fact, Nazarbayev dissolved the parliaments in Kazakhstan in December 1993 and in March 1995, primarily because they did not support his policies on economic reform. Nazarbayev subsequently ruled by presidential decree from March 1995 to December 1995. During this period significant reform legislation was implemented, including a revision of the tax code to adhere to international standards, and legislation allowing banks to operate more independently from the government. As a result of the economic program envisioned for 1996–98, the IMF approved an advanced loan for Kazakhstan in 1996 and noted that 1995 had been the most successful year for the Kazakh economy.[8] Nazarbayev was able to proceed with economic reform by manipulating the political system in order to bring in supporters of his economic reform policies and to remove his opponents.

In contrast, Uzbekistan's governmental elite (also guided by Karimov) has shown remarkable continuity from the Soviet to the post-Soviet era. The post-Communist parliament has been as compliant as the parliament during the Soviet era in passing measures introduced by the government (Roeder 1994; Melvin 2000). Karimov did not have problems with his parliament because there was no apparent disagreement on his decision to proceed slowly with economic reforms or to delay reforms when the economic situation did not bring in needed revenue for the state. Olcott explains that "decisions made about the pace of privatization and other economic reforms are shaped in part by the personal interests of President Karimov, his inner circle, and a small group of other privileged regional elite" (2005, 120). In short, the leaders of the two countries may appear similar in some areas (Communist history, authoritarian style), but differences in their actions concerning the former Soviet elite are crucial to their decisions about economic reform.

For this study, the elite are defined as the group of people who hold the largest share of political and economic power. The relationship between the elite and the president will be examined based on whether the elite supported a president's economic policies. One way to measure the power of the elite is to examine the extent to which there has been personnel turnover in key economic sectors or government positions (Hellman 1998, 229). Specific indicators used to determine the degree of influence of the elite will include whether there has been a continuation of economic policies followed during the Soviet era, and the frequency in turnover of state and government officials. This latter component has been used by other scholars to measure the elite in Kazakhstan.[9] My study seeks to extend the analysis of the elite by additionally framing its interests as they relate to the Soviet past. This analysis provides a clear trajectory and basis for predicting advancement or delay of economic reform.

## Economic Reform and Investment

As explained in the first section of this introduction, macroeconomic reform as the dependent variable will be examined in three areas: progress on privatization, price liberalization, and progress in reforming the trade and foreign exchange system. These are important measures of progress for countries transitioning from planned to free-market economies because they are indicators of the economic freedom of markets, as opposed to the control of economic policies by the government (Fischer and Sahay 2000; Gleason 2003a; Åslund 2007). Policies enacted to create market economies should also lead to the establishment of legal and regulatory frameworks to support those policies. For example, procedures to privatize formerly state-owned assets require rules and regulations about the sale and transfer of those assets. On the other hand, if the privatization of state-owned assets does not occur and they remain in the control of the government, there is no need for policies governing their sale and transfer. Consequently, if the government is dominant in the economy, there is less need for these legal frameworks.

Improvement in macroeconomic conditions is expected to lead to increased investment and business in the transition economies. Indeed, in the CEE and Baltic states significant correlations have been found between progress in economic reform, the establishment of a legal and regulatory framework, and increased foreign investment in those states (Meyer 1998; Michalet 1997; Bevan and Estrin 2004; Jensen 2006). Different reform paths followed by Kazakhstan and Uzbekistan also explain, in part, the different foreign investment in the two states. Cumulative FDI into Kazakhstan from 1993 to projections for 2005 were over US$19 billion; Uzbekistan's cumulative amounts for the same time period were US$1.3 billion (EBRD 2005, 19).

## Overview and Structure of the Book

In the early part of an interview with an IMF economist, I explained that I wanted to examine differences in the economic reform policies of Uzbekistan and Kazakhstan. His response was that I would be examining differences between "a tortoise and a hare."[10] What was so surprising to me about his comment was that there was nothing in the political science literature that would have predicted it. There was little work on the differences between the former Soviet republics because political scientists and some economists had grouped them together as later reformers (except for Kyrgyzstan).[11] In this volume I present evidence for Uzbekistan's lack of progress on reforms and Kazakhstan's advancement on reforms based on conditions and experiences from the Soviet past.

The book will proceed as follows. Chapter 1 examines how each republic's level of integration with Soviet-era Russia in areas such as infrastructure, geography, and natural resource endowments has affected reform in each country. Kazakhstan had an economy highly integrated with Russia that constrained its ability to operate at the same economic level after independence. Uzbekistan did not depend on a system integrated with Russia to function at the same economic level after independence, which is one factor in the government's decision to halt reforms.

The next chapters focus on political and leadership variables and how they have influenced reform in Uzbekistan (chapter 2) and Kazakhstan (chapter 3). Each chapter begins with an analysis of the elite, including the continuity in persons in the Uzbek government from November 1992 to 2005, and the turnover in persons in the Kazakh government from November 1992 to October 1995. These chapters show that differences in progress on economic reforms largely occurred during two important periods. In Uzbekistan, economic reform was delayed or reversed in 1996–97 as a result of dramatic increases in prices of the products the country imported (wheat and consumer goods) and declines in the cotton harvest, which the government relied on as the primary earner of export revenues. The country also implemented the distorted exchange rate regime in the latter part of 1996 to control the country's terms of trade. Conversely, in Kazakhstan, economic reform was advanced during Nazarbayev's rule by presidential decree and without a parliament from March to December 1995. My discussion of economic reform includes excerpts from speeches and published documents by Presidents Nazarbayev and Karimov to illustrate their differing views on market-oriented policies.

Chapter 4 examines the relationship between the implementation of reforms and foreign investment and business decisions in the two countries. I conducted interviews with U.S. representatives whose firms had invested or conducted business in one or both countries during September–October 2003, with follow-up interviews conducted in May 2005. These interviews demonstrate a link between the specific areas of reform that each country implemented and the volume and type of investment deemed important by U.S. investors.

The final chapter summarizes the main findings and speculates about the future reform efforts of Kazakhstan and Uzbekistan.

# 1

# Breaking Apart from Russia

The Soviet system was designed to benefit Russia, and Russia's relationships with the other Soviet republics were based on the resources that each could provide it. The republics had varying levels of economic integration with Russia, and thus differing constraints on the choices available to their leaders at independence. This chapter will examine how Kazakhstan's and Uzbekistan's integration with, and proximity to, Russia in geography, infrastructure, and disposition of natural resources has affected economic reform in each country. In part because they share a geographic border, Kazakhstan's economy was highly integrated with Russia's, an arrangement that limited Kazakhstan's ability to operate at the same economic level after independence. The economy of Uzbekistan, on the other hand, was less integrated with that of Russia, giving it greater economic freedom after independence. This relative freedom, added to President Karimov's decision to continue policies on cotton production that began during the Brezhnev era, is one factor in the Uzbek government's slower progress along the path of economic reform.

## Economic Integration with Russia: Geography and Resources

### KAZAKHSTAN

The most obvious geographic difference between Kazakhstan and Uzbekistan is that the former borders Russia, while the latter is located further south. Kazakhstan's

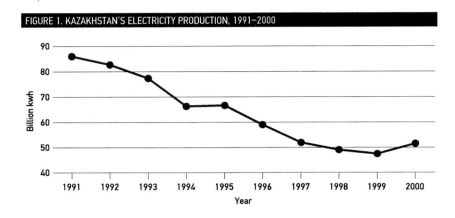

FIGURE 1. KAZAKHSTAN'S ELECTRICITY PRODUCTION, 1991–2000

proximity to Moscow explains why it was treated much more favorably than the other Soviet republics in areas such as investments in infrastructure. Kazakhstan received higher than average funding, which resulted in industrial development in metallurgy, machine building, and heavy and light industry (Brukoff 1995). In turn, Kazakhstan's electrical sector, coal production, and oil and gas pipeline systems were structured to support Russia. The following paragraphs provide a brief account of this asymmetrical relationship in the energy sector.

First, Kazakhstan did not have a unified electrical supply system during the Soviet era. Its electrical sector was divided into two main grids: in the north and the west, a grid that was connected to the Russian system, and in the south, a grid that was connected to the rest of Central Asia. Kazakhstan lacked independent control over these weakly connected electrical grids and suffered interruptions that were one cause of the drop in electrical production in Kazakhstan after the end of the Soviet system (see figure 1).

Declines in production were also the result of Kazakhstan's policies. In the initial stages of economic reform, a rise in energy prices resulted in decreases in domestic demand and declines in output (World Bank 1993a, 112–13). In addition, because of the country's unpaid debts to Russia, Moscow cut off power to Kazakhstan's northern factories soon after its independence (Olcott 1998, 100).

Second, Kazakhstan was the third largest coal producer in the Soviet Union, and about 40 percent of its production was exported to Russia (World Bank 1993a, 111). The multiple-track railway line built in the 1930s to transport coal to Russia indicated the importance of the Karaganda field, located in eastern Kazakhstan, as a supplier for Russian industry. The Karaganda field was crucial to the Soviet Union as the main supplier of coking coal for the metallurgical industries of the Urals.

After the end of the Soviet Union, Kazakhstan's production of coal dropped significantly, declining 39 percent from 1991 to 2001 (ISCCIS 2002, 51). The decrease was due to many factors, including restructuring of the sector, high tariffs for the use of Russian rail systems, and price increases resulting from decreased demand (World Bank 1993a, 113; IMF 1996, 6–7). Production of coking coal (coking is the process used to make coal suitable for the manufacture of steel) in particular declined steadily after independence, and from 1997 to 2000 all of its exports of coking coal went to Russia, as opposed to the Baltics and the other FSU (former Soviet Union) states (see figure 2) (IMF 2002, 95).

Kazakhstan's continued export of coking coal to Russia was in part the result of rail tariffs imposed by other republics and their lack of resources to pay for coking coal. But it is a stark example of an area of economic integration of these two republics that emerged from the Soviet era.

Finally, Kazakhstan did not have a unified oil and gas pipeline system during the Soviet era. The two main refineries are Pavlodar in the northeast and Shymkent in the southeast, while the main oil deposits are in west Kazakhstan, bordering the Caspian Sea. Kazakhstan's crude oil was exported to Russia for refining, while Kazakhstan's refineries were designed to refine crude from Siberia via the Omsk-Pavlodar-Shymkent pipeline (World Bank 1993a, 8). Kazakhstan has sizable reserves of crude oil, but lacks a connected pipeline and refinery system to refine and export it. Estimates made soon after independence placed

FIGURE 2. KAZAKHSTAN'S EXPORTS OF COKING COAL TO THE BALTICS, RUSSIA, AND OTHER FSU STATES, 1993–2000

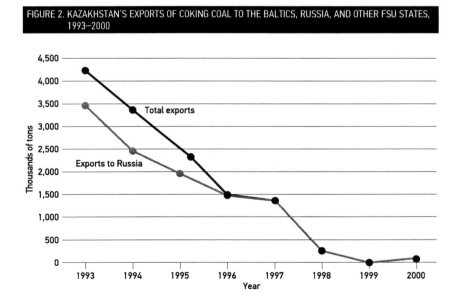

Kazakhstan's recoverable oil reserves at 12 billion barrels, and the country ranked second in oil production among the FSU states (after Russia) (World Bank 1993a, 8). Recent estimates put Kazakhstan's proven and recoverable reserves much higher, at 30 billion barrels, and the Kashagan field alone is thought to have reserves of 13 billion barrels.[1]

Russia was so well integrated with Kazakhstan because it wanted to control and take advantage of its natural resources. Their shared border made integration in these areas of infrastructure much easier to achieve. After the dissolution of the Soviet Union, the government of Kazakhstan decided that it could not operate within Russia's integrated system, and would have to engage the international community to increase international involvement in sectors formerly intertwined with the Russian economy. This decision is evident in steps taken to engage outside investors for oil pipeline structures and projects, as well as in the privatization of large enterprises in the power and gas sectors. Outside investors were needed for their expertise and for funding the maintenance and repair of outdated Soviet infrastructure.

For example, in 1998 six out of 13 international consortia of oil firms involved in oil and gas field projects in Kazakhstan were engaged in the construction or repair of oil pipelines (Dittmann, Engerer, and von Hirschhausen 2001, 141). This outside investment was required for Kazakhstan to increase its output of oil as an independent state.[2] Astonishingly, Kazakhstan's oil production grew from 25.8 million tons in 1997 to 68.7 million tons in 2007 an increase of 62 percent.[3] As a result of the development of new fields and increased oil production, the country will likely be one of the top 10 oil-producing nations in the world within the next 10 years (Kaiser and Pulsipher 2007).

### UZBEKISTAN

While Uzbekistan is also endowed with natural resources, it depended on Russia for the production and export of those resources less than did Kazakhstan during the Soviet era.

Uzbekistan was the third largest producer of natural gas in the Soviet Union behind Russia and Turkmenistan. Since Russia had large reserves of gas, most of the Uzbek production was used domestically for local industry; only about 8 percent was exported to Russia, primarily to the Urals through the Bukhara pipeline (World Bank 1993b, 4). Uzbekistan has its own internal gas lines as well as large reserves. In contrast to the Nazarbayev government in Kazakhstan, the Karimov government did not strongly pursue foreign investment to develop new infrastructure to exploit natural gas resources for export shortly after

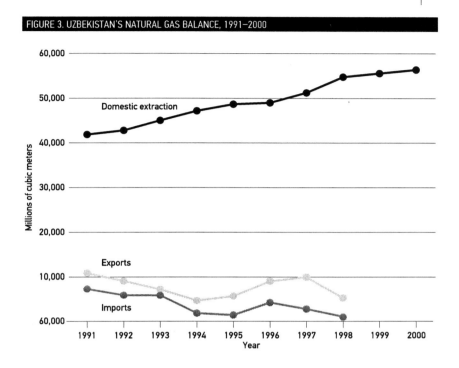

FIGURE 3. UZBEKISTAN'S NATURAL GAS BALANCE, 1991–2000

independence. Instead, the county increased domestic production and decreased both imports and exports of natural gas (see figure 3).

For two reasons, this relative independence in energy production is important for understanding the early trajectory of the economic reform process in Uzbekistan. First, the country's self-sufficiency in energy is one of the reasons for the country's slow decline in output relative to the other FSU states (Zettlemeyer 1998). Second, the Uzbek government did not develop a framework designed to attract foreign investors to assist in upgrading the country's natural gas infrastructure until 2004, because the gas was needed to maintain domestic industry and was still subsidized by the state. As of 2008, the government was still setting domestic prices for basic food items and energy, subsidizing these goods for Uzbek citizens (IMF 2008a, 8). The Uzbek government's eventual turn to outside investment in its natural gas industry can be explained by the simple fact that production was barely keeping up with consumption by 2002 (see figure 4).

The Russian firm Gazprom negotiated agreements in May 2004 and in September 2008 with Uzbekistan to build pipelines to transport gas from Uzbekistan and Turkmenistan to Russia, ostensibly to be re-exported to Europe.[4] Additionally, in June 2004 the Russian firm LUKoil reached an agreement to

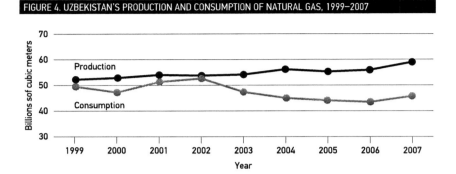

FIGURE 4. UZBEKISTAN'S PRODUCTION AND CONSUMPTION OF NATURAL GAS, 1999–2007

develop Uzbekistan's gas fields, two of which (Kandym and Gissar) are expected to produce 12 billion cubic meters of gas annually.[5] The government of Uzbekistan viewed the agreements with the Russian government as beneficial since Uzbek gas will be bought by Russia at world market prices. It is likely that the Russian government was interested in this agreement primarily for geopolitical reasons (as opposed to economic ones), specifically to increase its alliances within its former sphere of influence, thus limiting future Western oil and gas projects in the region.[6] This strategy has become even more of a concern for Russia following the heated military conflict with Georgia in August 2008.

Uzbekistan was a substantial producer of gold during the Soviet era, producing about one-third of the total of the entire Soviet Union (World Bank 1993b, 4–5). While gold and oil are both natural resource commodities, an important difference between the two is that a country's ability to export gold does not depend on an infrastructure system (such as pipelines) to transport the resource to the market. Further investments were needed to increase gold mining beyond levels of production reached in the Soviet era, but mining operations prior to independence were already such that Uzbekistan was the eighth largest producer of gold in the world (Commodity Research Bureau 2000, 111). Uzbekistan was able to increase its gold production by 22 percent from 1992 to 2005 (according to estimates for that year), providing an important source of revenue for the government since gold is sold for dollars on the world market (Commodity Research Bureau 2003, 111; 2007, 113).

In fact, gold is the country's largest export commodity, followed by cotton. The Uzbek government did (reluctantly) pursue outside investment in production of gold, but again, this was a source to generate external revenue. There were no harmful effects on the domestic economy or the domestic population in increasing gold production for export.

However, policies affecting the agricultural sector in Uzbekistan, specifically a focus on cotton production during the Soviet era, did affect the domestic population and economic structures of the country.

First, Uzbekistan's total area employed for agriculture increased more than any other Soviet republic from 19.2 million hectares in 1949 to 26.6 million hectares in 1958 (Committee for World Atlas of Agriculture 1969, 488). The agricultural sector in Kazakhstan was important too, but it would not have the continuing effects on the republic that were evident in Uzbekistan. The main reason was that the Virgin Lands campaign begun by Khrushchev in the 1950s to grow grain in the Kazakh steppe was largely a failure and was discontinued in the 1970s (Gilbert 2002, 136). The contributions of the Uzbek republic, unlike Kazakhstan, were concentrated in the agricultural sector.

While Uzbekistan is primarily noted for its cotton growing, it was also the largest producer of fruits and vegetables within the Soviet Union (World Bank 1993b, 5). The total production of fruits and berries for the six highest producing oblasts of Uzbekistan in 1970 was a little over three million tons (3,352,000) (Uzbek SSR Tsentral'noe statisticheskoe upravlenie 1971). The most recent comparable data indicate that the production of fruits and berries fell to only 660,000 tons in 1986 (World Bank 1993b, 285). The production of these agricultural crops, traditional to Central Asia, was decreased because of the focus on cotton production (Rumer 1989, 71). A comparison of the production of these two agricultural crops of Uzbekistan illustrates how the agricultural sector in Uzbekistan was fundamentally altered during the Soviet era. Indeed, Uzbekistan was transformed into an economy focused entirely on cotton production—a cotton monoculture. Table 1 shows the increases in the production of raw cotton in the seven largest producing oblasts in Uzbekistan from 1960 to 1970.

The total production of raw cotton by the seven highest producing oblasts in 1970 was a little over three million tons (3,072,000). Cotton production hovered around 5 million tons annually until 2004–5, when it increased again to over 5 million. Estimates for 2007–8 were at 5.5 million tons (Commodity Research Bureau 2008, 65). This output has made Uzbekistan the fifth largest cotton producer in the world.

There were three primary reasons that Uzbekistan was viewed as an ideal republic for the purpose of cotton production during the Soviet era, and all of these factors would in turn greatly influence the development of post-Soviet Uzbekistan. First, it has a favorable climate. Cotton requires sun during the growing and flowering season, a lack of very cold weather, and an abundant water supply (Rumer 1991, 62–63). Uzbekistan's climate had these features,

| TABLE 1. PRODUCTION OF RAW COTTON IN THE SEVEN HIGHEST PRODUCING OBLASTS IN UZBEKISTAN, 1960–1970 (IN THOUSANDS OF TONS) | | | | |
|---|---|---|---|---|
| OBLAST | 1960 | 1965 | 1969 | 1970 |
| Tashkent | 249 | 353 | 317 | 380 |
| Syrdarya | 284 | 441 | 460 | 576 |
| Fergana | 323 | 465 | 453 | 495 |
| Samarkand | 311 | 382 | 365 | 443 |
| Bukhara | 218 | 314 | 402 | 469 |
| Kashkadarya | 144 | 194 | 272 | 302 |
| Khorezm | 265 | 352 | 330 | 407 |

SOURCE: Data compiled by the author from *Uzbekistan za gody vos'moi piatileki* (1966–1970gg), 1971.

except for adequate rainfall. Rainfall averages about fifteen inches annually, but only about three inches fall during the cotton-growing season of mid-June to mid-August (Rumer 1991, 62–63). Therefore, in order to 'facilitate' the additional water needed for cotton growing, vast irrigation systems were developed during the 1960s around the natural waterways of the Amu-Darya and the Syr-Darya, the two largest rivers that feed into the Aral Sea.

These irrigation projects resulted in a devastating 50 percent decline in the Aral Sea's surface area between 1960 and 1996 (World Bank 2001, 3). The deterioration of this body of water has resulted in worsening environmental and health problems for both Uzbeks and Kazakhs, since both countries border the Aral Sea.[7] If better irrigation systems were developed, they would be more efficient and water quality would improve, resulting in increases in the fish population and lower levels of salinity. By comparison, Kazakhstan has made progress in updating its irrigation systems, in part from a loan through the World Bank (World Bank 2001). The decision of the Kazakh government to update its irrigation methods is largely attributed to a drop in agricultural production, which resulted in a decision to privatize the sector.[8] The agricultural sector, on the other hand, is a major source of income for the Uzbek government.

A second reason to grow cotton in Uzbekistan is demographic. Cotton production is extremely labor intensive, and Uzbekistan is the most populous of the Central Asian republics. As a result of the specialization in cotton production, the country actually had larger shifts of the population from some of the urban to the rural areas in the seven highest cotton-producing oblasts in the 1960s.[9] As a country develops economically, the opposite usually occurs: population shifts from the rural to the urban areas, as people move to the cities for employment in the nonagricultural sector. The fact that the population in cotton-growing oblasts was moving from urban to rural areas to supply the additional labor needed to produce cotton shows the state's focus on cotton production. This trend continued after the 1960s, and by 1991 the rural population was 59.9 percent of the total, the urban population 40.1 percent (World Bank 1993b, 253). By 2000 the urban population was 37.3 percent of the total; the figure decreased slightly to 36.7 percent by 2005 (UNESCAP 2006, 56). Agriculture is still a primary sector of employment, accounting for 30 percent of employment and 22 percent of the country's GDP in 2007 (World Bank 2008). Uzbekistan has a growing working age population, and if agriculture were reformed to reflect more modern methods of production, employment would likely decrease in the agricultural sector, contributing to social instability. Raw cotton is still purchased by state-owned firms at fixed prices and then sold at world market prices, generating revenue for the state.[10]

Third, the type of cotton that Uzbekistan grew was also dictated by Soviet ideas that valued quantity over quality. The country primarily grew upland (short staple) cotton, as opposed to pima (long staple) cotton during the Soviet era, and continues to do so.[11] Differences in the length of the strain determine the worth of the cotton; the longer the strain, the more it is worth.[12] Therefore pima cotton is used for higher quality and higher priced textiles, while upland cotton is used for lower quality textiles. Upland cotton also has a shorter growing season than pima cotton, producing higher yields. Pima cotton requires less water than upland cotton but has a longer growing season. The Soviets decided to pursue the cotton that would produce higher yields even though it would require extensive irrigation. Thus, the evolution of Uzbekistan's economy into a cotton monoculture was based on its specialization in production of a particular type of cotton that demanded disastrous irrigation techniques. It is hard to overstate how these developments would affect economic and political life in post-Soviet Uzbekistan.

Kazakhstan and Uzbekistan were similar in some aspects of their integration with Russia during the Soviet era in that both provided natural resources to Russia. However, Russia used these resources in different ways and made more of an effort to integrate Kazakhstan's resources with its own. This was done for practical and administrative reasons, including building rail systems and moving Russians to the northern part of the republic during the Virgin Lands campaign. Uzbekistan's economic ties with Russia during the Soviet era differed in that the same effort to integrate its resources was not made. Uzbekistan was a primary cotton grower, but not a primary textile manufacturer. There are some secondary cotton manufacturing oblasts in Uzbekistan (Fergana and Tashkent), but the primary manufacturing oblasts (Ivanovo and Kostroma) are located near Moscow. Boris Rumer (1989, 12, 73) has explained that the decision by the Soviets to ship cotton fiber to Moscow, and then to reship manufactured textiles back to Central Asia, was designed to regulate the development of certain regions, not on sound economic principles.

## The Brezhnev Era

Policies pursued during the Brezhnev era (1964–82) complemented the geographic and resource integration already established between Kazakhstan and Russia, and further isolated Uzbekistan from Russia. The Brezhnev era is an important period for understanding policies implemented in Kazakhstan and Uzbekistan because the Communist Party leaders of each republic had a great deal of discretion in their decision making. Soviet policy during this period focused on consensus, stability, and job security for the elites (Bunce and Echols 1980, 8–13). As long as the Soviet elite was able to meet economic planning goals (of primary importance in a command economy), job security for the elite was assured.

Dinmukhamed Kunayev served as the first secretary of the Kazakh Communist Party from 1960 to 1986. Kunayev had a great deal of influence on Kazak politics and leadership during his tenure as first secretary. He increased the participation of trusted Kazakhs, appointing them to important positions in Kazakhstan. Party leaders of the other Central Asian republics, including the leader of Uzbekistan, also appointed members of their titular ethnic group to important positions during the Brezhnev era. However, Kunayev was unique in that he also appointed Russians.

This decision can be attributed to the fact that there were higher numbers of Russians in Kazakhstan than in the other republics, as a result of previous efforts, including the Virgin Lands campaign, to settle Russians in the republic. In fact, for most of Kazakhstan's history the Kazakhs were a minority in their own republic and the Russians a plurality. Kazakhs did not comprise a plurality in Kazakhstan until 1989 (with 40 percent of the population, while Russians still made up 38 percent) (CIA 1995). However, Kunayev's actions were also taken for practical political reasons, including a drive to integrate Kazakhstan and Russia. Indeed, Kunayev's actions meant that policies of ethnic separatism, while still practiced in the wider Soviet system, were no longer widely practiced in Kazakhstan (Olcott 1995, 246).

Politics and nationalistic issues in Uzbekistan during the Brezhnev era took a markedly different turn. Sharif Rashidov served as the first secretary of the Uzbek Communist Party from 1959 to 1983. Rashidov had the greatest impact on Uzbekistan through his implementation of three events: the facade of increases in cotton production, the increase of Uzbek officials in key government and party organizations, and a continued focus on the virtues of Uzbek nationalism. In keeping with the policies of the Brezhnev era, Rashidov was allowed to run the republic as he wished as long as he met his economic planning goals; this meant increasing the amount of cotton sent to Moscow. The data provided by the Uzbek republic indicated that cotton deliveries to Moscow met or exceeded planned targets from 1978 to 1983.[13] However, the amounts of cotton actually delivered were much lower, and estimates are that Moscow paid more than four billion rubles for cotton that was never delivered.[14] In this sham production, known as the "Cotton Affair," reported amounts of raw cotton delivered to Moscow were inflated, either by bribing officials at the procurement centers (where the cotton was delivered) or by increasing the area where cotton was cultivated, and concealing this increase from the statistical agencies (see Rumer 1989, 70–71). Falsifying the amount of raw cotton delivered was required primarily because the targets set by Moscow were unrealistic. They were unrealistic because, despite the huge increases in arable land, Uzbekistan had reached its limits of production. By the mid-1970s and early 1980s,

> Fertile soils [had] been deleted, and the acreage under cultivation [had] reached its absolute outer limits, given the available water supplies. Yet Moscow, operating as ever on the principle that one must surpass the "attained level," constantly [raised] the plan targets. There remain[ed] but one alternative: inflation of the data. (Rumer 1989, 71)

To succeed with this deception Rashidov had to set up a network of officials whom he could trust to go along with false data on cotton production. While most of these officials were Uzbek, the inflation of amounts delivered to Moscow could not have been accomplished without the help of Russian officials. This was confirmed when Brezhnev's son-in-law Yuriy Churbanov was linked to the Cotton Affair and, with other executives of the Uzbekistan Interior of Ministry, tried for corruption.[15] The Cotton Affair would severely damage relations between Uzbekistan and Russia because it was perceived very differently in Moscow by Russians than in Uzbekistan by Uzbeks. Moscow told a story of horrible crimes of corruption and bribery, while in Uzbekistan the prosecution was seen as an unfair prosecution of Uzbeks. Indeed, many of the officials involved used the diverted funds for their local communities for necessary projects that were unauthorized by Moscow (Critchlow 1988; 1991a). In February 1991, Karimov "rehabilitated" or cleared Rashidov and other Uzbek officials involved in the Cotton Affair.[16]

While the policies under Rashidov would have a significant impact on Uzbekistan, they really did not come to light until after Gorbachev's election as premier in 1985. Gorbachev's drive to end the corruption that had gone unchecked during the Brezhnev era began with a campaign to purge the republic's elites. However, his policy to replace corrupt officials was met with resistance in both republics.

On December 15, 1986, the first party secretary in Alma-Ata (then the capital of Kazakhstan) was fired for abuses of power, and seven of 19 local Communist officials were replaced. Ominously, Soviet specialists predicted that this move would "likely tarnish the image of Kunayev . . . as one of the last influential politicians of the Leonid Brezhnev era."[17] The next day, Kunayev was "released" from his position, and Gennadii Kolbin, a Russian, was chosen as his replacement. Gorbachev's determination to put an end to corrupt elite networks likely influenced his decision to promote a Russian and not a Kazakh. However, the decision to appoint a Russian as the leader of the Kazakh republic did not go over well, even though Kazakhs were a minority, and there was rioting in Alma-Ata in which several people were reported killed.[18] Nursultan Nazarbayev replaced Kolbin on June 22, 1989.

The policies of purging the elites were even more pronounced in Uzbekistan because Rashidov had promoted larger numbers of trusted Uzbek officials over Russians to important party and administrative positions.[19] Indeed, Rashidov's replacement in Uzbekistan, Inamzhon Usmankhodzhayev, was later accused of corruption in taking bribes and falsifying amounts of raw cotton procured.[20] Therefore, the purging of elites in Uzbekistan, coupled with the portrayal of those involved in the Cotton Affair, came to look much more like discrimination aimed at Uzbeks. Islam Karimov became the first party secretary of the Communist Party for Uzbekistan on June 23, 1989, one day after Nazarbayev assumed the same position in Kazakhstan.

The policies implemented by Rashidov and Kunayev affected each republic as it moved toward independence only to the degree that subsequent leaders continued those policies. In Uzbekistan, the focus on cotton production implemented by Rashidov was continued by Karimov in the post-Soviet era. In Kazakhstan, on the other hand, Nazarbayev largely disassociated himself from Kunayev and his policies, and he implemented economic policies designed to establish a more independent Kazakhstan. For example, in 1991, discussing the future implementation of unpopular economic measures that Kazakhstan would follow, Nazarbayev stated, "We will have to grit our teeth the whole way through. It was this way in Turkey and South Korea. Now they have built flourishing societies."[21] Karimov, in contrast, envisioned a different approach to economic reform. In 1991, in a profile piece on the present situation in Uzbekistan, he stated, "Shock treatment will not work in Uzbekistan. The Polish model will not work in Uzbekistan. . . . So I say that our specific features are special. From that point of view, we cannot agree to shock treatment."[22] Very early into independence the two presidents took different views on the appropriate path to economic reform. The end of the Soviet Union resulted in independence for both republics and an opportunity for both presidents to chart the economic reform of their respective countries. The following two chapters will examine the strategies each followed and the role of the elite, further explicating why Kazakhstan and Uzbekistan followed different paths to reform.

# 2

# Agreeing to Manage Economic Policies in Uzbekistan

slam Karimov had no intention of moving quickly to implement economic reform policies after the dissolution of the Soviet Union. Members of the former Soviet elite continued to hold power with Karimov as president, an arrangement that shaped the country's path of reform in two related ways. First, reforms were delayed in order to protect the political and economic interests of the elite and to maintain social stability. This delay is most evident in the lack of reform in the cotton production sector, a clear holdover from the Rashidov era. President Karimov (unlike President Nazarbayev) evidenced no disagreement with his government on the decision to proceed slowly with economic reforms, or to put them on hold when the limited initial reforms did not bring in adequate revenue for the state. Second, the decision to implement the multiple exchange rate regime in 1997 was made out of economic necessity. The government needed more control over the economy in order to pay for necessary imports, including wheat and goods for industry, and to compensate for steep declines in revenue derived from the country's primary exports.

## Karimov's Early Background

Islam Abduganievich Karimov was born in 1938 in Samarkand, Uzbekistan (Vronskaya and Chuguev 1992, 120). His political career was different from that of most Communist Party officials (including Nazarbayev) because he did not rise up through the Communist Party hierarchy by holding prominent positions. Instead, Karimov was able to consolidate power through a turn of events surrounding the failed attempt to overthrow Gorbachev in 1991.

In one of his earliest positions, Karimov was the first party secretary of the rather remote Kashkadarya oblast, in December 1986.[1] Even though this was not a very important political position, being in charge of this isolated area served as a symbolic position for Karimov because "this form of political exile marked him as a man with a grievance against the Moscow-installed leadership and gave him experience in the CPSU elite, albeit in a backwater region" (Carlisle 1995, 196). During this time Gorbachev was carrying out his campaign to purge the elite leadership, and he had just replaced the previous first secretary of the Uzbekistan Communist Party, I. Usmankhodzhaev, with Rafik Nishanov. Nishanov was then viewed as part of the "Moscow-installed leadership" (much as Gennadii Kolbin was viewed in Kazakhstan, as described in the previous chapter). Karimov replaced Nishanov as first secretary on June 23, 1989. While Karimov came into Uzbek politics as a relative outsider, he soon brought back many of the older former Soviet elite, mainly from the Rashidov era. However, Karimov first engaged in a struggle with the influential people that helped bring him to power.

Shakarulla Mirsaidov was one of those influential people, representing the elite from the Tashkent region of Uzbekistan. Mirsaidov had previously held a position as the chair of the Tashkent City Soviet Executive Committee and had served as mayor of Tashkent for five years.[2] Mirsaidov was influential in having Karimov promoted to his position as first secretary, and when the Supreme Soviet elected Karimov president in March 1990, Mirsaidov was made vice president.[3] However, the two men did not get along, and Karimov looked for a way to solidify his power against Mirsaidov.[4] The coup attempt in Moscow provided Karimov with the opportunity that he was looking for.

When the coup attempt was reported in Moscow in August 1991, Karimov was in India on an official trip.[5] Reaction among the republics to the coup attempt varied. Uzbek authorities called for order, and the perception in Uzbekistan was that they favored the coup attempt against Gorbachev believing that his policies were going to lead to the breakup of the Soviet Union; which Mirsaidov and his allies opposed. However, these actions were organized by Mirsaidov and his allies, as Karimov was in India. Therefore, as Donald Carlisle explains, "there is reason to believe that the emergency measures imposed in Tashkent were independently taken—perhaps by Mirsaidov and his allies—before Karimov took charge. The failure of the coup thus weakened his enemies in the Tashkent establishment, not Karimov" (1995, 198).

When Karimov was elected president during the general election on December 29, 1991, he was able to solidify his power by decreasing the importance of the vice president, and he eventually abolished the position altogether. William Fierman's research supports the suggestion that Karimov and Mirsaidov were engaged in a power struggle. According to Fierman (1997, 378) Mirsaidov traveled to Moscow in September soon after the declaration of independence, in an attempt to gather supporters in opposition to Karimov. Karimov's decision to marginalize and eventually oust his former supporter may have also been the result of a power struggle between competing clans in Uzbekistan (Collins 2004b). Mirsaidov and his allies represented the Tashkent region, while Karimov represented the Samarkand region. Notably, Rashidov and Ismail Dzhurabekov (whose position in the early government will be discussed below) also represented Samarkand. Thus, Karimov's decision to rehabilitate Rashidov and other officials involved in the Cotton Affair resulted in the return of many of the policies and the members of the Rashidov-era elite. The following sections explain how Karimov's economic training and background additionally shaped his decisions regarding economic reform policies in Uzbekistan.

Karimov's training and education was primarily that of a Soviet economist; he held a position as the head of Uzbekistan's branch of the Gosplan agency in 1986.[6] Karimov's background in economics and with Gosplan greatly influenced his ideas about the path his country should follow in economic reform. For example, instead of disbanding Gosplan as the official economic planning agency, it was simply transformed into the Uzbek Committee for the Economy, and its analysts performed the same economic planning and development tasks carried out under Gosplan.[7] Indeed, an official with the Embassy of Uzbekistan stated to me that Karimov's economic background would allow him to understand the disadvantages of the shock therapy approach to economic reform.[8]

Statements made by Karimov at the beginning stages of independence are also key to understanding his views on economic reform. In many of his early interviews and writings he explained that a free-market economy was not appropriate for Uzbekistan. In an interview that Karimov gave to Moscow's *Izvestiya* on September 18, 1991, he explained that Uzbekistan was not ready for a market economy and that he would follow the Chinese model of limited economic reforms and would, like the Chinese, restrict political demonstrations. He stated further that he was not interested in political reforms similar to those that had been implemented by Gorbachev because "controlling and curtailing Communist Party activity today means throwing the economy into chaos."[9] Karimov's published writings likewise advocated a gradual pace of economic reform. In one of his early books, published in 1993, he explained that the transition from a planned economy to a market-based one would take time and should take place in successive phases. In a recent book, *Uzbekistan on the Threshold of the Twenty-First Century* he explained that an important component of the Uzbek model of market reforms would involve state regulation, arguing that "it is difficult to provide a smooth transition from any administrative-command system to the principles of a market economy when the regulating role of the state is ignored" (1998, 115–16).

It should have come as no surprise, then, that Karimov would continue the state-controlled economy. He was trained as a Soviet-style economist and stated in speeches and writings that his country should undertake only limited political and economic reform. Karimov also emphasized the threats to security that Uzbekistan consistently faced and, thus, the need for a balance between safety and economic reforms. "Threats to Security" is the title of the first part of *Uzbekistan on the Threshold* (Karimov 1998). Issues of security increased in importance with assassination attempts on Karimov, the rising influence of the Islamic Movement of Uzbekistan (IMU), and the Taliban's seizure of power in Afghanistan. The need for an increase in military expenditures was part of the justification for the decision to restrict imports and access to foreign exchange beginning in 1996–97.[10]

### The President and the Elite: The Early Uzbek Government and Early Reforms

The analysis of the elite as represented by the state and government officials appointed by President Karimov will illustrate two trends. First, there has been continuity among the elite in the Karimov government. One way to measure the power of the former Communist elite is to examine the extent of personnel turnover in key economic sectors or governmental positions appointed by the president (Hellman 1998). The Constitution of Uzbekistan, under Article 93, section 9, gives the president the power to "Appoint and dismiss the Prime Minister, his First Deputy, the Deputy Prime Ministers, the members of the Cabinet of Ministers of the Republic of Uzbekistan, the Procurator-General of the Republic of Uzbekistan and his Deputies, with subsequent confirmation by the Oliy Mazhlis."[11] Second, Uzbekistan personnel in key governmental positions were often members of the former Soviet elite; would often be trusted by the president to hold more than one position; and many would continue into present governmental positions.

## TABLE 2. UZBEK STATE OFFICIALS, PRE- AND POST-SOVIET PERIODS

| OFFICIAL | POSITION IN NOVEMBER 1992 | SOVIET ERA POSITION |
|---|---|---|
| Abdulkhashim Mulatov | Prime minister; chair, Committee for Reception and Distribution of Foreign Humanitarian Aid | |
| Ismail Dzhurabekov | First deputy prime minister | First deputy chairman, Uzbek president's Cabinet of Ministers* |
| Pulat Nugmanov | Deputy prime minister; minister of installation, special construction work | Minister of installation and special construction work** |
| Alikhan Atadzhamov | Deputy prime minister; minister of labor | |
| Bakhtyar Khamidov | Minister of economy; chair, State Committee on Prognostication and Statistics | Deputy chairman, Uzbek president's Cabinet of Ministers* |
| Inom Iskandarov | Minister of construction materials industry | Minister of construction materials industry** |
| Utkir Sultanov | Minister of foreign economic relations | |
| Kudratilla Mahamadalyev | Minister of construction (October 1993) | Minister of construction** |

SOURCES: Russia and Eurasia FFA 1992, p. 46–47; Russia and Eurasia FFA 1993, p. 517–520; Tashkent, *Pravda Vostoka*, in Russian, March 31, 1990, p. 1 in FBIS, April 16, 1990, p. 137.
* September 1991. The formal title of the cabinet was Committee for the Operational Management of the USSR National Economy.
** Council of Ministers, April 1990.

This is a very different situation from that found in Kazakhstan (covered in the next chapter), in which there is a lack of persons from the former Soviet elite continuing in key governmental positions. Differences between the continuity or change in the elite explain part of the progress or delay on economic reforms in the two countries.

The important persons and positions in the early Uzbek government are listed in table 2. As the table shows, many tops officials in the Soviet era continued on in the same capacity after independence, likely because of their relationship with Karimov before the dissolution of the Soviet Union. Inom Iskandarov's name is first noted in Foreign Broadcast Information Service reports in November 1987. He is listed as the deputy chairman of the Uzbek USSR Council of Ministers, as well as chair of the Uzbek branch of Gosplan.[12] Since Karimov was trained as an economist and had worked for Gosplan for a number of years, Karimov almost certainly came into contact with Iskandarov during this time. Iskandarov was first appointed as the minister of the construction materials industry in 1992. An additional person from the Soviet era, Kudratilla Mahamadalyev was appointed to the position of minister of construction in 1993. Previously, Mahamadalyev was deputy chairman of the Uzbek Council of Ministers, having been appointed in February 1986.[13] The continuation of these two men from the Soviet era into the early Karimov government indicates an important trend. Karimov appointed persons to important positions either because he trusted them or needed their support to solidify his political power base.[14] Since both Iskandarov and Mahamadalyev were members of the Uzbek Council of Ministers during 1986–87 (Karimov was part of the council in 1986), Karimov believed that he could trust them.

Ismail Dzhurabekov also held positions in Uzbekistan during the Soviet era. In 1991, he was the first deputy chairman of the Uzbek president's Cabinet of Ministers. Previously he had been a member of the Rashidov government, in the position of agricultural vice prime minister.[15] In 1992, Dzhurabekov was appointed as first deputy prime minister.

With this portrait of continuity from the Soviet era to independence having been drawn, we may now review the beginning stages of economic reform in Uzbekistan.

### EARLY ECONOMIC REFORMS

In 1994, Karimov (and his government) began to make important decisions about economic reform. Significant progress in systemic reforms was made after the presidential decree "Measures to Further the Economic Reforms, Ensure the Protection of Private Property, and Develop Entrepreneurship," issued on January 21, 1994. This decree advanced the privatization program to medium and large enterprises and contained a new law on foreign investment (IMF 1995, 13). However, economists with the European Bank for Reconstruction and Development (EBRD) noted that this mass privatization process may have resulted in the concentration of ownership "in the hands of insiders (workers and management)," likely hindering a more efficient restructuring of enterprises (EBRD 1995, 16). While advancement in the privatization of small enterprises was evident by 1995, the decision to postpone privatization in the energy and telecommunications sectors was judged by the EBRD as likely to hinder investment in those sectors because privatization in the latter sectors is also needed to facilitate private sector development as well as for overall future economic growth (EBRD 1995, 16).

The foreign exchange system in Uzbekistan underwent significant changes in 1994. The country's currency, the sum, became a convertible currency for some transactions, but with limitations. For example, by January 1994 restrictions on foreign exchange into and out of the country were removed, but limits were placed on the amount of foreign exchange residents could buy from authorized banks from Uzbekistan. In July 1994 the amount was US$250, in August it was increased to US$1,000, but by December the limit was reduced to only US$300 (IMF 1995, 39). Further limitations on foreign currency were put in place through a resolution passed on November 15, 1994, decreeing that "30 percent of foreign currency proceeds subject to compulsory sale by enterprises and establishments, irrespective of their form of ownership, are to remain as a whole at the disposal of the Central Bank of the Republic of Uzbekistan."[16] These restrictions are further evidence that the Uzbek government proceeded with some economic liberalization while keeping the state in firm control of the economy.

Foreign trade liberalization was also accelerated in 1995. The number of product categories subject to export quotas was reduced in early 1995 from seventy to eleven, although cotton and gas still had export quota and export-licensing restrictions since these products comprised more than half of the country's nongold exports (EBRD 1995, 63). By the end of 1995 there were only four products that had export quotas and had to go through export-licensing systems: cotton, oil, and ferrous and nonferrous metals (EBRD 1996, 183). Again, even though the overall number of products had been reduced, restrictions remained on goods deemed important to the state.

However, Uzbekistan had made enough progress on economic reforms by late 1994 to be approved for a Stand-by Arrangement (SBA) from the IMF on December 18, 1995. The SBA is a conditional lending facility from the IMF and is specifically designed to assist with stabilization policies. The IMF noted that the objectives for the economic program for October 1995–December 1996 (SBAs are usually from one to two years) were to consolidate "the gains made so far in macroeconomic stabilization, and to lay the foundation for economic recovery and improved living standards." The IMF stated that these objectives would be achieved by "accelerating market-oriented reforms and *reducing administrative interventions in the economy*."[17] This loan by the IMF to support Uzbekistan's 1995–96 reform programs was an important indicator of Uzbekistan's early progress on economic reform.

Analysis of the Uzbek government's early progress on economic reform shows three important trends. First, there was a remarkable degree of agreement between the president and the legislature in passing legislation and in issuing decrees on reform.[18] Second, Karimov used his authority as a strong leader to appoint persons from the former Soviet elite to important positions in his new government. These actions indicate a low turnover of the former Soviet elite.

Finally, Uzbekistan made some progress on economic reform in these early years, in important areas such as trade liberalization and decreasing the restrictions on export licensing and quotas. However, the government was still intervening to control goods deemed important to the state, such as cotton, grain, and gold. The government would effectively reverse gains previously made in economic reform during the latter part of 1996 and early 1997, primarily as a result of three events: decreases in the cotton harvest, increases in the price of wheat imports, and decreases in the world market price of gold.

## Delay of Economic Reforms

The first cause of delay was a significant decline in the cotton harvest in Uzbekistan in 1996. Output in the agricultural sector fell 7 percent largely as a result of adverse weather conditions for cotton growing. The summer months were not as warm as usual, and there were heavier than normal rains in September (IMF 1997b, 11). The gross harvest of raw cotton fell from 3.9 million tons in 1995 to 3.3 million tons in 1996 (ISCCIS 2002, 666). This was especially problematic because cotton exports were one of Uzbekistan's largest sources of revenue. The country's balance of payments situation from 1995–1997 would undergo significant changes, primarily as a result of the poor cotton and grain harvests in 1996 (see table 3).

The second problem that affected the balance of payments was an increase in the price of wheat imports, from US$153 a ton in 1995 to US$251 a ton in 1996, an increase of 64 percent (see table 3). During this period, Uzbekistan was trying to increase its grain production to achieve self-sufficiency and decrease its dependence on importing food. The government's plan was to shift some agricultural production from cotton to grain in order to achieve this objective. Indeed, from 1994 to 1998, the country's outputs of raw cotton decreased by 18 percent, while the production of wheat increased by 61 percent.[19]

Third, the world market prices for cotton and gold also steadily declined from 1995 prices (see table 3), resulting in decreased revenue for the state. Therefore, the situation in 1996 was a combination of "stagnating exports, high prices for grain imports because of a poor grain harvest in the region, and rapid growth in imports of consumer and investment goods [which] put pressure on the balance of payments" (IMF 1997b, 6). This led the authorities to implement further restrictions on imports and access to foreign exchange in mid-1996 in order to protect foreign exchange reserves.

**TABLE 3. UZBEKISTAN'S BALANCE OF PAYMENTS, 1995–1997 (IN US$ MILLIONS)**

| YEAR | 1995 | 1996 | 1997 |
|---|---|---|---|
| Current account | −21 | −980 | −584 |
| Merchandise trade balance | 237 | −706 | −72 |
| Exports | 3,475 | 3,534 | 3,695 |
| Cotton fiber | 1,584 | 1,539 | 1,390 |
| Gold | 611 | 906 | 738 |
| Energy | 436 | 277 | 528 |
| Other | 844 | 813 | 1,039 |
| Imports | −3,238 | −4,240 | −3,767 |
| Foodstuff | −618 | −1,252 | −786 |
| Energy products | −53 | −45 | −23 |
| Machinery | −1,151 | −1,542 | −1,868 |
| Other | −1,415 | −1,402 | −1,091 |
| *Memorandum items:* | | | |
| Price of cotton exports (US$/ton) | 1,754 | 1,592 | 1,582 |
| Price of wheat imports (US$/ton) | 153 | 251 | 223 |
| World gold price (US$/ounce) | 384 | 388 | 331 |

SOURCE: Republic of Uzbekistan: Recent Economic Developments IMF Staff Country Report No. 98/116, p. 109. IMF listed sources: Ministry of Finance, Ministry of Macroeconomics and Statistics (Government of Uzbekistan) and Fund staff estimates.

In November 1996 the IMF suspended the rest of the installments of the SBA because of Uzbekistan's continued allocation of too much financial support to the agricultural sector. The goals for the economic program developed by the Uzbek authorities for the SBA included objectives such as "reducing administrative interventions in the economy"; in the area of structural reform objectives included "further disengagement of the Government in economic activity."[20] Any negotiations that the Uzbek authorities may have had with IMF officials are not public information. However, an IMF economist very familiar with the situation stated that if the Uzbek government had consulted with the IMF regarding the balance-of-payments situation, the IMF could have negotiated different terms.[21] Instead the Uzbek government broke the performance criteria agreed upon, and the IMF had no option but to suspend the SBA.

In January 1997, Uzbekistan implemented a formal multiple exchange rate regime. This decision has been continually cited as one of the most damaging for the country's economy.[22] A primary purpose of this type of exchange rate system is to use "an overvalued official exchange rate to tax exporting sectors (cotton and gold) in order to subsidize imports of capital and priority consumer goods" (IMF 2000a, 7). The regime established several exchange rates, with the rate determined by the purpose of the transaction. The "official" rate was established through a system of administrative transactions including the exchange of proceeds from exports that were required for turnover to the government. The "auction" rate was used for transactions that were allowed access to foreign exchange, such as some imported inputs and investment goods. A separate "commercial" rate was used for the import of specific consumer goods and services, and finally the foreign exchange bureau of eligible banks for transactions with individuals used a cash market rate. However, the number of banks eligible for these types of transactions was reduced in 1997 from fourteen to only two (EBRD 1997, 212). The primary purpose of the multiple exchange rate regime was to give the government more control over the economy, even in areas that otherwise seemed to be out of the government's control.

## Continuing to Manage Economic Policies

One of the purposes of this chapter is to examine the continuity of the former Soviet elite as part of an explanation for decisions about managing economic reform. The premise is that there was a higher degree of agreement about decision making in the Karimov government because Karimov appointed to key positions persons whom he either knew or trusted (many from the Soviet era) because they shared his belief that Uzbekistan should chart its "own model for transition." The fact that individuals from the early 1992 Uzbek government continued as governmental officials into the late 1990s, and some even into the 2005 government, is a strong indicator of the continuity of some of the former Soviet elite, as depicted in table 4.

The other trend that is evident from table 4 is that Karimov still seems to have considerable power in shifting or removing persons in the government based on economic performance. The reason that Dzhurabekov and Khamidov were both gone from the government at roughly the same time (and why Sultanov was moved) is most likely related to the continuing gap between target amounts and the actual cotton harvest. In November 1998, the Projections and Statistics Committee projected that the cotton harvest would again fall at least 12 percent below the targeted amount (REFFA 1999, 424). The cotton harvest target had been missed in 1997 by almost 10 percent. Dzhurabekov and Khamidov had been

## TABLE 4. IMPORTANT UZBEK OFFICIALS AND POSITIONS IN THE GOVERNMENT, 1992–2005

| NAME / TIME IN KARIMOV GOVERNMENT | POSITION(S) | TOTAL YEARS SERVED |
|---|---|---|
| Erkin Khalilov 1994–2005 | Chairman Oliy Majlis, 1994–present | 11 |
| Utkir Sultanov 1992–2005 | Minister Foreign Economic Relations, 1992–Jan 1998; Deputy Prime Minister 1995; Prime Minister 1996–2003; First Deputy PM 2003–present | 16 |
| Ismoil Dzhurabekov 1991–1998 | Agricultural Vice Prime Minister; (Rashidov government); First Deputy Chair, President's Cabinet of Ministers, 1991; First Deputy Prime Minister, 1992–Nov 4, 1998; Minister of Emergency Situations, Dec 1996–Jan 1998; (new Ministry) Minister of Agriculture, Water Utilization, Nov 1998 | 7 |
| Bakhtyar Khamidov 1991–2000 | Minister of Economy, (changed to Minister of Finance in 1994) 1992–Dec 1999; Chair Committee of Prognostication and Statistics Deputy Prime Minister, 1994–July 28, 2000; Minister of Finance 1994–Dec 1999 | 9 |
| Elyor Ganiyev 1998–2005 | Minster Foreign Economic Relations Jan 1998–present | 7 |
| Fayzulla Mullajanov 1994–2005 | Chairman State (Central) Bank 1994–present | 11 |
| Rustam Azimov 1999–2005 | Minister of Finance (Dec) 1999–2000; Minister of Economy (combined with Macroeconomy and Statistics Ministry) 2003–2005; First Deputy Prime Minister 2005 | 5 |
| Oqiljon Obidov 1995–2005 | Minister of Labor Oct 1995–present (changed to Minister of Labor and Social Security 2004) | 10 |

SOURCES: Russia and Eurasia FFA, various years; http://uzland.narod.ru/gov.htm various years.

appointed to important positions in the Uzbek government, but Karimov often shifted or removed persons in the government based on economic performance. Dzhurabekov resigned his position as first deputy prime minister and as minister of agriculture and water utilization on November 4, 1998, most probably as a result of the poor cotton harvest. Khamidov, who served as both the minister of finance and minister of macroeconomics and statistics, was removed from those posts and appointed the new governor of the Kashkadarya region on the same date, July 28, 2000.

Clearly, economics and finance are important ministries in the Uzbek government. This is due to the unique economic situation of the country, in that it still operates very much as a command economy and, related to this, Karimov's early training in economics and his belief that he has the economic background to set the best course for Uzbekistan's reform policies. According to interviews with an economist from the IMF and with an official from the Embassy of Uzbekistan in Washington, D.C., confirmed that the most important ministry in making decisions regarding economic reform was the Ministry of Macroeconomics and Statistics.[23] Therefore, it appears that Khamidov was removed from his position because he was blamed for poor decision making with regard to reform. Interestingly enough, the next person assigned to this position, Rustam Shoabdurakhmanov, only held this position until January 2003, when the Ministry of Macroeconomics and Statistics was combined with the Ministry of the Economy; and was filled by Rustam Azimov, who currently holds the position and was first brought into the government in 1999.[24]

Another important economic ministry is the Ministry of Foreign Economic Relations, which controls almost all formal matters of trade. The responsibilities of this ministry include "negotiating trade agreements with non-traditional trading partners (outside the former Soviet bloc) as well as those arrangements denominated in hard currency with traditional trading partners, and for implementing foreign trade agreements and external trade policy through the issuance of licenses and export quotas" (IMF 1995, 34). This ministry has control over the export quotas and export-licensing restrictions on goods from Uzbekistan. In this important category fall goods, such as cotton and natural resources, that provide needed revenue for the state. Interviews with an economist from the IMF and with an official from the Embassy of Uzbekistan confirmed that the most important ministry for making decisions about cotton and decisions about other exported goods was the Ministry of Foreign Economic Relations.[25] Utkir Sultanov was the minister of foreign economic relations from 1992 until January 1998. Subsequently, Sultanov continued to serve in the government, as the prime minister through 2003 and then as deputy prime minister, his current position. Clearly he is still a trusted person in the Karimov government. Elyor Ganiyev became the minister of foreign economic relations in January 1998, following Sultanov, and currently serves in this position (see table 4).

Practices common during the Soviet era may also explain the pattern of changing or demoting of officials in the Karimov government. It was common under the Soviet system to remove or demote officials when their targets were not met. These shifts served both political and economic purposes in command or state-controlled economies: political because the system needs to punish those that have not fulfilled their obligations, and economic because unmet economic performance criteria in critical sectors damage the economy as a whole. Thus, we can surmise that political and economic components of decision making have played a role in the Karimov government. Ronald Wintrobe (1998) argues that it is necessary to analyze both of these components to understand decision making in a Communist economic system. He develops a bureaucratic system (as opposed to a market system) model to account for decisions in such a system, with political status being measured by the Communist Party's power: "the fundamental prediction of this model is . . . that in a Soviet-style system, there is a positive correlation between the power of the Party and measures of economic performance such as economic growth" (Wintrobe 1998, 217). Indeed, as table 4 illustrates, the longevity of the elite does not preclude the entry of new individuals into important economic positions.

These individuals came in to replace others during an economic crisis. These newcomers may have pushed for changes in economic policy, resulting in the implementation of the multiple exchange rate regime. At the very least, they went along with Karimov's decision to take this step. In an authoritarian government, a change in the elite does not necessarily mean a change in governmental policy.[26] While new people were brought in, the government's control over the economy increased, indicating a delay or, in fact, a reversal of reform policies. The implementation of the multiple exchange rate regime had the desired effects of giving the government more control over the economy. The government also increased its control over goods that could be imported during 2000 and 2002, according to IMF economists.[27] The fact that this distorted exchange rate system was kept in place until October 2003 indicates that the government did not wish to proceed with further economic integration until circumstances were favorable. Indeed, according to IMF economists, the government finally agreed to currency convertibility only when there were improvements in economic performance criteria. These criteria included a decrease in inflation below 20 percent and a satisfactory level of foreign reserves. The higher level of foreign reserves was also in part the result of higher world market prices for cotton and gold, which allowed for a stronger balance of payments situation.[28]

## The Future of Reform

Uzbekistan officially ended its multiple exchange rate regime in October 2003 by accepting Article VIII of the IMF's Articles of Agreement. A country notifies the IMF when it is ready to accept Article VIII obligations, and the Executive Board of the IMF then votes to make the information available on the IMF website.[29] Article VIII, sections 2, 3, and 4, designates that the member will avoid restrictions on current payments, avoid discriminatory currency practices, and agree to the convertibility of foreign-held balances.[30] While Uzbekistan's decision to accept these obligations was described as a "positive" step in progress on economic reform, economists from the IMF also stated that more extensive reform would be needed in the future, including the lifting of trade restrictions.[31] Unfortunately, Uzbekistan has made little progress in these areas.

For example, the European Bank for Reconstruction and Development announced in April 2004 that because of limited progress on political and economic benchmarks that the bank had outlined for the country in 2003, it could no longer be involved in financing projects with the government of Uzbekistan and would instead focus on projects that benefited Uzbeks in the private and public sectors. The report noted the following problems with regard to unmet economic benchmarks:

> Current-account convertibility of the Uzbek currency . . . has been introduced in line with Article VIII of the IMF Agreement. Yet the potential benefits of these steps are diminished by reported restrictions on access to foreign exchange for consumer imports and the tight cash squeeze on the economy. There has been progress in liberalizing the agricultural sector, with some increase in the state procurement price for cotton, but not to a market level. The tight cash squeeze has diminished the benefit of higher prices to producers.[32]

Further problems with currency convertibility for both households and enterprises were documented in a 2005 study on the effects of distortionary policies in Uzbekistan (Gemayel and Grigorian 2005). Problems that businesses have had with currency convertibility will also be addressed in chapter 4.

A country's progress in the area of current account convertibility and a decision to comply with a unified exchange rate is closely related to progress in the reform of the trade and foreign exchange system. Current account convertibility is an important indicator of a decreasing role for the government in the economy because currency convertibility means (among other things) that the currency is convertible at a rate set by the market and not by the government. Table 5 shows that even when the Uzbek government formally accepted currency convertibility in 2003, the rating of the indicator did not increase until 2005, and even then only increased marginally, which is indicative of the fact that the country did not have full account convertibility.

A comparison of Uzbekistan's progress with that of Kazakhstan's progress in the reform of its trade and foreign exchange system (see table 6) indicates two important differences in the reform processes of the two countries. While

| | TABLE 5. EBRD RATING OF TRADE AND FOREIGN EXCHANGE SYSTEM AND BENCHMARKS OF REFORM FOR UZBEKISTAN, 1991–2008 | | | |
| --- | --- | --- | --- | --- |
| YEAR | EBRD RATING | | YEAR | EBRD RATING |
| 1991 | 1.00 | | 1999 | 1.00 |
| 1992 | 1.00 | | 2000 | 1.00 |
| 1993 | 1.00 | | 2001 | 1.67 |
| 1994 | 2.00 | | 2002 | 1.67 |
| 1995 | 2.00 (first Stand-by Arrangement) | | 2003 | 1.67 (currency convertibility) |
| 1996 | 2.00 | | 2004 | 1.67 |
| 1997 | 1.67 (SBA suspended) | | 2005–08 | 2.00 |
| 1998 | 1.67 | | | |

CLASSIFICATION SYSTEM FOR TRANSITION INDICATORS: TRADE AND FOREIGN EXCHANGE SYSTEM

1. Widespread import and/or export controls or very limited legitimate access to foreign exchange.

2. Some liberalization of import and/or export controls; almost full current account convertibility in principle but with a foreign exchange rate regime that is not fully transparent (possibly with multiple exchange rates).

3. Removal of almost all quantitative and administrative import and export restrictions; almost full current account convertibility.

4. Removal of all quantitative and administrative import and export restrictions (apart from agriculture) and all significant export tariffs; insignificant direct involvement in exports and imports by ministries and state-owned trading companies; no major non-uniformity of customs duties for non-agricultural goods and services; full current account convertibility.

The classification system is simplified and builds on the judgment of the EBRD's Office of the Chief Economist. The previous system used '+' and '–' rankings added to the 1–4 scale in 1997 to indicate countries on the borderline between two categories (EBDR 1997, 15)

NOTE: The classification system for the transition indicator scores has been modified from previous reports. Previous '+' and '–' ratings are treated by adding 0.33 and subtracting 0.33 from the full value. Averages are obtained by rounding down, for example, a score of 2.6 is treated as 2+, but a score of 2.8 is treated as 3– (EBRD 2007). These changes were made by the author for ease of comparison.

SOURCE: EBRD 2008.

both have accepted Article VIII obligations, Kazakhstan did so much earlier than Uzbekistan (1996), and the country has not placed restrictions on its currency, as has been the case in Uzbekistan. This difference is in Kazakhstan's ratings by the EBRD for this indicator, which have been consistently higher than Uzbekistan's.

The EBRD noted the lack of progress on political reform as part of the reason that it was limiting its involvement with the Uzbek government. Benchmarks that had not been met included the official registration of opposition parties and nongovernmental organizations (NGOs) that concentrated on the rule of law and the protection of human rights.[33] The human rights in question included the right to peacefully demonstrate against the government, which became an even more pressing issue as a result of the government crackdown on protestors against the government during May 2005 in Andijan. Indeed, the protestors were demonstrating in part against the poor economic conditions in the country, although the government blamed Islamic extremists for the uprising.[34]

The most recent presidential elections in Uzbekistan were held on December 23, 2007, with Karimov winning 88 percent of the votes cast. The Office for

TABLE 6. EBRD RATING OF TRADE AND FOREIGN EXCHANGE SYSTEM AND BENCHMARKS OF REFORM FOR KAZAKHSTAN, 1991–2008

| YEAR | EBRD RATING | YEAR | EBRD RATING |
|------|-------------|------|-------------|
| 1991 | 1.00 | 1998 | 4.00 |
| 1992 | 1.00 | 1999 | 3.33 |
| 1993 | 2.00 | 2000 | 3.33 |
| 1994 | 2.00 (first Stand-by Arrangement) | 2001 | 3.33 |
| 1995 | 3.00 | 2002 | 3.33 |
| 1996 | 4.00 (currency convertibility; | 2003 | 3.33 |
|      | Extended Fund Facility) | 2004 | 3.67 |
| 1997 | 4.00 | 2005–08 | 3.67 |

CLASSIFICATION SYSTEM FOR TRANSITION INDICATORS: TRADE AND FOREIGN EXCHANGE SYSTEM
1. Widespread import and/or export controls or very limited legitimate access to foreign exchange.
2. Some liberalization of import and/or export controls; almost full current account convertibility in principle but with a foreign exchange rate regime that is not fully transparent (possibly with multiple exchange rates).
3. Removal of almost all quantitative and administrative import and export restrictions; almost full current account convertibility.
4. Removal of all quantitative and administrative import and export restrictions (apart from agriculture) and all significant export tariffs; insignificant direct involvement in exports and imports by ministries and state-owned trading companies; no major non-uniformity of customs duties for non-agricultural goods and services; full current account convertibility.

NOTE: The classification system for the transition indicator scores has been modified from previous reports. Previous '+' and '–' ratings are treated by adding 0.33 and subtracting 0.33 from the full value. Averages are obtained by rounding down, for example, a score of 2.6 is treated as 2+, but a score of 2.8 is treated as 3– (EBRD 2007). These changes were made by the author for ease of comparison.

SOURCE: EBRD 2008.

Democratic Institutions and Human Rights of the Organization for Security and Cooperation in Europe (OSCE/ODIHR) assessed the elections (common practice for former Soviet republics), but for two reasons sent a Limited Election Observation Mission. First, because visas for the mission were not granted until November 26, it was impossible to observe and assess the conditions of the elections in a timely manner (OSCE 2007, 1). Second, as the OSCE/ODIHR report noted, "the apparent limited nature of the competition" made a comprehensive assessment of the procedures on election day unnecessary (OSCE 2007, 6). The elections were clearly not designed to allow anyone but Karimov to win the presidency. It was technically illegal for Karimov to run again according to the Uzbek constitution, since he had already served two consecutive terms as president. However, as long as the elite continue to benefit from and support his policies on managed economic reform, he may end up presiding over the country until his death.

Because of its managed approach to economic reform, Uzbekistan will suffer relatively little from the worldwide financial crisis that emerged in 2008. First, the country did not liberalize its financial markets and thus did not engage in or depend on investment or trade in these areas with the international community, apart from deals with Russia for natural gas exports. Second, when financial crises occur and strong currencies lose their value, investors buy gold to supplement their portfolios, a boon to exporters of the metal, such as Uzbekistan. The price of gold has been steadily increasing since 2002 (it fell from 1997 to 2001). The average price increased from US$310.13 an ounce in 2001 to US$363.51 in 2003 (also the year of currency convertibility Uzbekistan) and then rose to US$604.00 for 2006 (Commodity Research Bureau 2008). The future price of gold was projected to be US$1114.50 (per ounce) for April 2010.[35] Uzbekistan will likely continue to increase its revenue from exports of gold.

A potential problem area is residuals from the economic crisis. Even though Uzbekistan reports high economic growth, the poverty rate decreased by only 1.7 percentage points from 2001 to 2005, and was 25.8 percent of the population for 2005, according to the World Bank. Uzbek citizens (like citizens from many countries) have had their incomes supplemented by remittances from labor migrants in Russia and Kazakhstan, which the World Bank estimates at 8–12 percent of the country's GDP for 2005–7.[36] As these laborers return home in response to the economic downturn, they will put extra strain on the government to provide for their employment. According to the 2007 Welfare Improvement Strategy of Uzbekistan, the Ministry of Labor and Social Protection was responsible for creating "not less than 550,000 new jobs every year for 2008–2010."[37] However, it is more likely that the government will simply place greater restrictions on imports and the levels of foreign exchange (as it did in the earlier economic crisis), as opposed to making drastic changes in economic production. In fact, the Soviet-style state order system is still in place for cotton and wheat. This means that a percentage of cotton and wheat produced by farmers must be sold to the government at a price lower than the world market price. The government then sells the goods for the world market price and keeps the difference (in economic terminology, the "rents"). It is widely believed that the elite in the Uzbek government benefit from this system in that they keep a share of these rents.[38] While there could also be another government shakeup (Oquilijon Obidov as the current minister of labor and social protection should be the most concerned about meeting the job creation targets), the partial and "gradual" approaches to economic reform have been in place far too long for any radical shifts to emerge now, especially from a government headed by Karimov.

# 3

# Economics Determines Politics for Nazarbayev

Nursultan Nazarbayev quickly implemented reforms designed to move Kazakhstan toward a market economy beginning in January 1992. Nazarbayev did not have the same close relationship with the former Soviet elite that Karimov had, and disagreed with them over how to proceed with economic reform. Kazakhstan progressed on reform as a result of decisions, made in large part by Nazarbayev, to disband noncompliant parliaments where much of the power of this elite was concentrated in December 1993 and March 1995. From March to December 1995 Nazarbayev ruled by presidential decree and during this period initiated political and economic changes designed to consolidate his power. He had a new constitution adopted by referendum in March that gave the president much more power than the previous constitution, adopted in 1993. Exercising his powers of presidential decree, he reformed banking and the tax code and liberalized trade. Nazarbayev was able to proceed with these economic reforms by manipulating the political system, removing his opponents in order to bring in people who would support his policies.

## Nazarbayev's Early Background

Nursultan Abishevich Nazarbayev was born in 1940 near the former capital of Almaty and was employed as a steelworker at the Karaganda metallurgical combine.[1] Nazarbayev (unlike Karimov) rose up through the ranks of the

Communist Party in Kazakhstan, holding prominent positions, including party secretary at the Karaganda combine. His subsequent positions included secretary of the Central Committee of the Kazakh Communist Party in 1979; chairman of the Council of Ministers of the Kazakh SSR from 1984 to 1989; first secretary of the Central Committee of the Kazakh Communist Party, 1989; and member of the Politburo of the Communist Party of the Soviet Union in 1991 (Vronskaya and Chuguev 1992, 357). This type of political history generally indicates a close relationship with the Soviet elite, and Nazarbayev did have a close relationship with Gorbachev. However, Nazarbayev began to distance himself from the elite as early as 1991 with statements that there should be no Communist party influence on economic strategy when the elite disagreed with him on the implementation of economic reform policies.

Nazarbayev replaced Gennadii Kolbin as the first secretary of the Kazakh Communist Party in Kazakhstan on June 22, 1989.[2] Recall from chapter 1 that Kolbin (a Russian) had replaced Dinmukhamed Kunayev (a Kazakh) during Gorbachev's drive to rid the Soviet Union of the corrupt elite. Indeed, Nazarbayev was likely surprised that he himself was not chosen to replace Kunayev: he had developed a good relationship with Gorbachev, was a prominent Kazakh in the Communist Party, and had been critical of Kunayev's policies while he was first party secretary.[3]

The tumultuous relationship between Kunayev and Nazarbayev is surprising in that the former was responsible for Nazarbayev's promotion from party secretary in Karaganda to the position of chair of Kazakhstan's Council of Ministers (Olcott 1995, 259). Nazarbayev first began to criticize Kunayev in February 1986, citing among other inadequacies his poor "methods of administration" (Alexandrov 1999, 6–10). In a speech given in March 1986, Nazarbayev cited the need for improvement of the "negative phenomena" that had affected the republic's national economy, which he attributed to "serious failings and shortcomings in the leadership of the economy . . . and violations in the principles of social justice as well as in the selection, placement and training of cadres."[4] Nazarbayev's attacks on Kunayev gradually increased, and by November 1986, Kunayev was describing him as a "dangerous man" and told Gorbachev that he must be stopped. Mikhail Alexandrov's (1999, 6–10) account of the relationship between the two men shows that each worked to undermine the other, arguing that Nazarbayev's motives were political and that he believed distancing himself from Kunayev was a way to move into a more powerful political position. In an interview in April 1990, Nazarbayev admitted to criticizing Kunayev:

I dared to openly criticize D. Kunayev, member of the Politburo, at our party congress. I shall say honestly that I did this after agonizing over it, according to my convictions, remembering who he was and believing that, all the same, time would provide the most correct assessments of him. And my criticism of him was constructive and to the point.[5]

Nazarbayev had a critical view of Kunayev and his policies while Kunayev was the first party secretary. His early actions to distance himself from Kunayev made it easier for him to proceed more independently of the former Soviet elite than for Karimov in Uzbekistan. For example, during an interview that Nazarbayev gave in April 1991, he stated that "the trouble with Kunayev the cadre party member is that he is a son of his times." Conversely, during the same interview, when asked about his relationship with Gennadii Kolbin, Nazarbayev confirmed that he talked with him often and stated that he believed that Kolbin "wanted honestly and conscientiously to do something, to make changes for the better—I can say that firmly.[6]

Nazarbayev's statements on the path that Kazakhstan should take toward economic reform also differed from those of Karimov. Nazarbayev declared as early as 1991, "We have to transform our economy to a market economy as fast as possible."[7] Nazarbayev realized that he would need to create a new economy within a new framework in order to move Kazakhstan forward as an independent country.[8] He rejected a continuation of the influence of Communist ideology on economic change: "I believe that we must resolutely separate the economy from ideology. There should be no party influence on economic strategy including influence by the Communist Party."[9] Nazarbayev chose a greater degree of integration with the world community along internationally accepted standards. Kazakhstan, like Ukraine and Belarus, had nuclear weapons on its territory as part of the Soviet Union's nuclear stance, and voluntarily gave up those weapons and the country's status as a nuclear power. There had been underground testing in Kazakhstan, predominately in the area of Semipalatinsk, resulting, according to reports, in miscarriages and premature births. A strong antinuclear movement arose in the Semipalatinsk region, which was certainly reason enough for Nazarbayev to push for a nuclear-free state.[10]

A second reason for the decision to give up nuclear weapons involved Kazakhstan's place in the international community. In his book *Epicenter of Peace*, Nazarbayev stated that the "possession of nuclear weapons cannot be a stimulus for the development of external integration. In conditions where we could potentially flex our nuclear muscle from time to time, there could be no thought of civilized integration into the world community" (Nazarbayev 2001, 50). There was also a great deal of pressure from the international community, especially from the United States, for Kazakhstan to give up its arsenal, leaving only Russia with nuclear weapons. Nazarbayev and then Secretary of State James Baker discussed the special relationship that Kazakhstan had with the United States and in May 1992, Kazakhstan signed the START Protocol, which allowed nuclear capabilities to be located only in Russia.[11] Kazakhstan then signed the Nuclear Non-Proliferation Treaty in December 1993, and in return for this decision, the United States provided a total of $84 million and agreed to help Kazakhstan with its denuclearization process (REFFA 1994, 376–77). His statements and actions indicate that Nazarbayev wanted to integrate Kazakhstan within the international community early in his country's independence.

President Nazarbayev began his administration largely with state and government officials who had been in place during the Soviet era. However, the state and government officials appointed by Nazarbayev illustrate a trend toward new individuals in positions of power. Specifically, there were substantial changes in key economic sectors and governmental positions appointed by the president.

The first constitution passed by the Supreme Soviet in January 1993 accorded a fair amount of power to the legislature. The legislature was a unicameral body with 360 members and functioned along the lines of a parliamentary system, with the addition of a president—a semipresidential system, as it were. Disagreements over how much power the parliament should wield relative to the president were present as early as November 1993, and would result in a political crisis in May 1994. The 1995 constitution changed the government to a presidential system, with parliament holding greatly reduced powers.

In Kazakhstan, personnel in key governmental positions were not members of the former Soviet elite, none of whom continued in governmental positions; the president also trusted some key persons to hold more than one position. This is a key difference from the continuity of the elite in the Karimov government. A change in the composition of the elite orchestrated by Nazarbayev is one reason Kazakhstan was able to implement policies of economic reform.

## The President and the Elite: The Early Kazakh Government and Early Reforms

Most of the officials in the early Kazakh government (the former Soviet elite) did not continue to hold positions of power. There were three primary reasons for their losing their roles. First, it appears that few of these officials had close relationships with Nazarbayev, like those that Karimov had with holdovers from the Soviet era. Second, even though many of the early officials were economists, they advocated a gradual approach to economic reform and liberalization that was in sharp contrast to the speed of change envisioned by Nazarbayev. Third, and related to the latter reason, the composition of the state and government officials was altered because of changes in the political and economic situation beginning in December 1993. Therefore, this is a very different situation than what occurred in Uzbekistan. The following sections will illustrate the similarities between the 1992 and 1993 Kazakh governments (under the noncompliant parliaments) and their contrast with the late 1994 and 1995 Kazakh governments (under the noncompliant and then nonexistent parliament).

Important persons and positions in the early Kazakh government are listed in table 7. Three persons who were part of the Soviet era elite were in the Kazakh government in 1990 and remained in 1992. Yerik Asanbayev was chair of the Supreme Soviet in October 1990, and when Nazarbayev was sworn in as president of Kazakhstan in December 1991, Asanbayev was made vice president, in addition to serving as the chair of the Commission for the Attraction and Use of Foreign Investments.[12] Uzakbai Karamanov was appointed prime minister of the Kazakh SSR in November 1990, and was listed as a state councillor in the 1992 government.[13] Asanbayev and Karamanov were both economists.[14] Finally, Oktyabr Zheltikov was appointed trade minister in June 1990 and was released from his prior position as deputy chair of the Kazakh SSR Council of Ministers.[15]

### EARLY ECONOMIC REFORMS

In 1992 and 1993 Kazakhstan began to implement certain market-oriented reforms. In January 1992 the prices of most goods were liberalized, except for bakery goods and bread, which were liberalized in October 1994 (EBRD 1995, 45). All other price subsidies were eliminated, except for tariffs on utilities including electricity, by October 1994. Kazakhstan's privatization program for the largest enterprises began in 1993; the privatization of medium-sized enterprises continued through 1995 (EBRD 1995, 45). EBRD economists noted in their analysis

**TABLE 7. KAZAKH STATE OFFICIALS, NOVEMBER 1992**

| NAME | POSITION |
| --- | --- |
| Yerik Asanbayev* | Vice president; chair, Commission for the Attraction and Use of Foreign Investments (chair of the Supreme Soviet, October 1990) |
| Myrzatai Dzholdasbekov | State councillor, deputy prime minister |
| Sydzyk Abishev | Member, Commission for the Attraction and Use of Foreign Investments; chair, Foreign Economic Relations |
| Daulet Sembaev* | Member, Commission for the Attraction and Use of Foreign Investments; first deputy prime minister |
| Sergei Tereshchenko | Chair, National Agency on Foreign Investment; prime minister |
| Kadyr Baykenov | Deputy prime minister; minister of energetics and fuel resources |
| Baltash Tursumbaev | Deputy prime minister; minister of agriculture |
| Gen. Sagadat Nurmagambetov | Minister of defense |
| Kanat Turapov | Minister of material resources |
| Uzakbai Karamavov* | State councillor; (Prime minister, Kazakh SSR, November 1990) |
| Oktyabr Zheltikov | Minister of trade (deputy chair of the Kazakh SSR Council of Ministers) |

NOTE: All officials listed except Dzholkasbekov and Sembaev held a government position in October 1993.
*Person was identified as being an economist.
SOURCES: REFFA 1993, 311–14; 1994, 377; , *Izvestiya* (Moscow), in Russian, November 22, 1990, p. 1, Foreign Broadcast Information Service, November 23, 1990, p. 54; *Sotsialistik Qazaqstan* (Alma-Ata) in Kazakh, June 6, 1990, p. 1, Foreign Broadcast Information Service, June 15, 1990, p. 132.

that Kazakhstan, unlike Uzbekistan, offered investors "significant minority interests" in its strategic sectors such as energy and telecommunications. It is important to note that countries that adopted such policies for the privatization of their strategic sectors included such advanced reformers as Hungary and the Czech Republic (EBRD 1995, 16). Kazakhstan also introduced its own currency, the tenge, on November 15, 1993. In the same month Nazarbayev submitted a resolution that would allow the president and government to speed up decisions on economic reform. This resolution was rejected by the Supreme Soviet, and thus began the rocky relationship Nazarbayev would have with parliament until the end of 1995.[16]

The main problem was that parliament consisted of the senior political elite, a group that did not want to move quickly to implement economic reform (see Olcott 1997, 220). The Speaker of the parliament, Serikbolsyn Abdildin (part of the nomenklatura elite), and Nazarbayev clashed on many occasions over the pace of reform (see Cummings 2005, 24–25; Furman 2005, 208–9). Indeed, the parliament did not view the advancement of reform as furthering their economic interests. Recall that the hypothesis explained in the introductory chapter found that a new leadership (meaning not former Communists and not left over from the Soviet era) was necessary to push through painful economic reforms was based upon the premise that the old elite benefited from the distorted economic policies of the old system and would not want to give up those advantages. Nazarbayev and some members of his government wanted to move quickly to implement market-oriented policies, although the legislature wanted to move much more slowly and to protect their economic interests. Cummings explains that "parliament also represented distinct economic interests which fiercely opposed an IMF-backed stabilization programme, something which Nazarbaev and the government of Tereshchenko had tried to push through since the beginning of 1993" (Cummings 2005, 25). Therefore, on December 10, 1993, Nazarbayev persuaded the Supreme Soviet, the parliament elected in March 1990 during the Soviet era, to pass two pieces of legislation. The first law, "On the Temporary Delegation of Additional Powers to the President of Kazakhstan and Local Chief Administrators," gave Nazarbayev the right to implement decrees that would have the force of law, a power that would end after the elections in March 1994 for a new parliament. The second law, "On the Early Termination of the Powers of the 12th Supreme Soviet of Kazakhstan at the End of Its 11th Session," basically dissolved the current parliament until the March elections. Nazarbayev took these actions because of his unhappiness with the parliament's progress on economic reform. Indeed, the Kazakh ambassador to Moscow, Tair Mansurov, would later categorize this parliament as "unwieldy" and "unable to function."[17] There is also speculation that Nazarbayev was following Russian president Boris Yeltsin's actions to dissolve the local soviets before "recommending" that the regional soviets dissolve themselves in October 1993. In November 1993 one local soviet in Almaty adopted a resolution to self-dissolve and encouraged other soviets to do the same, which they did, possibly leading to the decision on December 10, 1993, for the Supreme Soviet to self-dissolve.[18]

### THE 1994 PARLIAMENT AND THE TERESCHENKO GOVERNMENT

The second parliamentary elections since independence were held on March 4, 1994. Nazarbayev took a number of steps to ensure that this parliament would be more compliant than the last. The new parliament, the Supreme Kenges, would have a total of 177 seats, much smaller than the previous parliament of 360 deputies. Of these seats, the election law allocated 42 seats for candidates that voters would choose from a list of 64 nominated directly by Nazarbayev, called the 'presidents' list.' In other words, Nazarbayev chose a group of acceptable candidates, then voters decided from among them; managed democracy, if you like. The remaining 135 seats were filled through elections from the territorial constituencies. (CSCE 1994).

The official report from the Commission on Security and Cooperation in Europe (CSCE) about the election concluded that it could not be considered free and fair because the candidates from the 'president's list' were chosen in advance, there were instances of multiple voting, and the campaign was brief, lasting only from December 1993 until March 1994. The response of the government was to defend the elections as democratic while noting that the proceedings correlated with the current level of democracy in Kazakhstan, with Nazarbayev explaining that the country was on its way to "reaching" European democratic standards (quoted in CSCE 1994, 13). Much of this discussion became irrelevant because the new parliament and the president would develop differences of opinion on economic reform early in their new relationship.

The first point of disagreement was the budget for 1994, which had been endorsed by presidential decree in January 1994. The Supreme Kenges stated that it would examine "the president's decrees adopted in absentia of the legislative body of power," referring to the time between the dissolution of the Supreme Soviet (December 1993) and the election of a new parliament (March 1994). Included in the examination was the budget for 1994.[19] On May 30, 1994, the Supreme Kenges issued a lengthy statement on the Kazakh Radio Network critical of the government's economic reform program, stating that the parliament "must express a lack of confidence in the government's social, economic and legal policy," in effect a vote of no confidence in the government.[20]

The Supreme Kenges believed that the government of prime minister Sergei Tereschenko was moving too fast on measures of economic reform and, specifically, that reforms needed to better protect the population. The day after the statement on the radio (May 31, 1994) the press service of the Cabinet of Ministers also released a statement through the Kazakh Radio Network. It declared that according to the constitution of 1993 the Supreme Kenges did not have the power to declare a statement of no confidence in the government, because according to the constitution, "the Cabinet of Ministers is answerable to the president of the republic." Second, the statement asserted that the government had been addressing social areas of reform:

> The government has submitted about 60 draft laws to the Supreme Kenges on
> urgent and topical issues of economic reform, law and order and others. Adoption of

these and other documents could have made it possible to improve the legal basis of the reform, to increase purpose-oriented social protection of the population.[21]

In a text released that same day, the government of Kazakhstan stated that it would "firmly" pursue a stringent financial policy, with a budget deficit target of no more than 4 percent of GDP for the year, the figure that it had agreed upon with the IMF.[22] Kazakhstan had concluded its first SBA with the IMF on January 26, 1994, of which this tight budget policy was a "key element."[23] Fundamentally, the government of prime minister Tereschenko was having the same problems with the new parliament that it had had with the old Supreme Soviet; the two bodies could not agree on the pace of reform policies or on the areas of reform that were most important.

The differences between the two parliaments, though, center on their motivations for pushing for slower reform. Members of the Supreme Soviet had acted to protect their own economic interests, while it seems that the democratically elected Supreme Kenges was responding to the concerns of their constituents who believed that economic reform was taking away the social welfare support that the state had provided under Communism. Indeed, remarks made by parliamentarian Marat Ospanov indicated that the parliamentarians had concerns about the impacts of these policies on ordinary Kazakhs. He stated that parliament

> should show the people that we are able to carry out our own policy. We should not comply with circumstances and, by doing so, bring more economic hardship and weaker social protection to our people. We should help to firm up our national currency. Prices are increasing. We should curb this growth. We should stop irreversible changes in the economy. This is our main concern and nothing else.[24]

However, the stalemate between the parliament and the government would not improve. On June 2 the press secretary of the government of prime minister Tereschenko stated again that the no-confidence declaration made by the parliament was unconstitutional and that the Tereschenko government was a capable governing body.[25] The tone in Kazakhstan had reached that of an economic and political crisis. The newly elected parliament with its statement of no confidence and a vote confirming such (although it was by a narrow majority) was effectively declaring that the government should resign. The Tereschenko government and Nazarbayev, by contrast argued that, according to the constitution, the government was responsible only to the president and that in effect the parliament needed to pass the legislation concerning the economic reform program that had been submitted by Nazarbayev.

By mid-June Nazarbayev himself became more involved in implementing changes in his government, most notably by removing some officials and making new appointments. Much of this activity can be explained by instances of corruption and abuse, resulting in Nazarbayev's decree titled "On Additional Measures to Ensure Legality and Law and Order" of June 14, 1994.[26] Kadyr Baykenov (a member of the 1992 government; see table 7) and Igor Ulyanov were both removed from their positions as ministers, and both of the ministries they had headed were abolished on June 14.[27] Another flurry of shuffling ministers occurred on June 17. On this date, Oktyabr Zheltikov was relieved of his position as minister of trade and Vyacheslav Kostychenko was appointed minister of Trade and Industry, a new ministry. Recall that Nazarbayev had appointed Zheltikov to this position in June 1990. The ministers of social protection and social security also resigned on this date; a presidential decree appointed five new officials on the same day and made changes in other ministries.[28] On June 22, Nazarbayev released a statement supporting the reorganization of the ministries and personnel changes because "new, younger people having a good idea of what business and economic reform are about have joined the Cabinet."[29] Nazarbayev explained that the government would have fifteen months to implement a new "anti-crisis policy program" and that if it could not be implemented, then the cabinet would resign.[30]

In September two members of the cabinet, Mars Urkumbayev, the minister of economics, and Vladimir Shumov, the minister of internal affairs, were charged with abusing their official positions and were relieved of their positions by presidential decree.[31] This scandal, added to the no-confidence vote, was too much to be dismissed, and on October 11, 1994, Nazarbayev asked for and received the resignation of Tereschenko and the entire Cabinet of Ministers.[32]

### THE 1994 PARLIAMENT AND THE KAZHEGELDIN GOVERNMENT

The parliament then approved the appointment of Akezhan Kazhegeldin as the new prime minister. Kazhegeldin had previously served as the first deputy prime minister in the Tereschenko government. Kazhegeldin was known for his "high level of competence in matters concerning organization of the economy," a clear reason that Nazarbayev would nominate him to be the next prime minister.[33] In fact, many persons from the Tereschenko government remained in the Kazhegeldin government, although their official positions changed. Altynbek Sarsenbayev and Akhmetzhan Yesimov both assume a new position as deputy prime minister, and Kasymzhumart Tokayev and Bulat Bayekenov also had new portfolios as minister of foreign affairs and minister of internal affairs, respectively. Sagadat Nurmagambetov was the only official who kept his previous position, as minister of defense. Indeed, he is the only person to continue in the Kazhegeldin government from the early 1992 government.[34] The fact that Nazarbayev reappointed some persons from the failed Tereschenko government is not surprising because it included ministers whom he trusted or who agreed with his economic reform plans.

Indeed, Nazarbayev seems to have placed a great deal of trust in Vladimir Shkolnik, who first appeared as minister of science and new technologies in the Tereschenko government. Shkolnik was then reappointed by Nazarbayev to serve in the Kazhegeldin government, and he would continue in subsequent administrations, serving as both minister of trade and minister of energy. Thus, while some key persons were trusted by the president to hold more than one position, this arrangement was much rarer than in the Karimov government in Uzbekistan. In addition, none of these officials served in the same governmental position during the Soviet era. Even Sagadat Nurmagambetov was no longer in the government in December 1996; he was the last official remaining from the early 1992 government (REFFA 1997, 281).

While Nazarbayev may have been happier with this new government, the parliament was not. In December 1994, it published a document critical of the performance of the Cabinet of Ministers, calling their fulfillment of the adjusted budget for 1994 "extremely unsatisfactory."[35] In what can only be called an interesting turn of events, the Kazakh Constitutional Court ruled on March 6, 1995, that the parliamentary elections held in March 1994 were invalid and that the parliament must dissolve.[36] The decision was not shocking, considering that international observers had not considered the elections to be completely free and fair. It is highly likely that Nazarbayev was at least somewhat responsible for the Court's decision. His subsequent decision to once again dissolve parliament was not unexpected since it was still "mounting opposition to his course of privatization and economic reform" (Olcott 1997, 227). Nazarbayev's comments following the dissolution of parliament argued that the constitution should be reformed so as to curtail the powers of the parliament.[37]

The People's Assembly of Kazakhstan became the president's new group with which to consult, absent a parliament. On March 24, 1995, the People's Assembly proposed extending Nazarbayev's mandate as president until the year 2000 (the next presidential elections were due to take place in 1996). In an address before the assembly, Nazarbayev described changes that would take place in the near future.

The executive branch of the government seems to be a tasty morsel to deputies because it has real power. The legislative power always traditionally encroaches on its functions. This causes conflicts that seem to an outsider to be the suppression of the legislative power by the executive power. But, in actual fact, this is the executive power's actions to protect itself against the legislative power's encroachments.

It is necessary to carry out constitutional reforms. A two-chamber parliamentary system is needed. Each branch of power should carry out its own business without encroaching on another's sphere of authority. If the practice of a tug-of-war emerges, if parliament becomes a political club for deputies to express themselves rather than a legislative body, there will be no tranquility in society.[38]

The following section will document important political changes that Nazarbayev undertook, as well as the advances in economic reform during his rule by presidential decree and without a parliament from March to December 1995.

### RULE BY PRESIDENTIAL DECREE: PROGRESS IN ECONOMIC REFORM

Nazarbayev's government and the various parliaments had differences of opinion on two components of reform going back to the beginning of the country's independence, one political and one economic. Political differences centered on the appropriate level of power and decision making that should be given to the executive branch. Nazarbayev had stated many times that he was unhappy with the power wielded by the parliamentary system of government and that Kazakhstan needed constitutional reforms. Thus, Nazarbayev focused on changing the constitution so that the majority of power would reside in the presidency, creating a semipresidential form of government.

However, in the discussion stages of the new constitution during June and July, not all Kazakhs were in favor of the increased role for the president. In fact, members of the Constitutional Court had sent Nazarbayev a confidential letter that was leaked to the public, explaining their belief that parts of the proposed constitution would be "undemocratic."[39] According to Igor Rogov, the vice chairman of the Constitutional Court, the concern was not that the executive branch would be strengthened; members of the court acknowledged that this shift of power would necessarily happen under a presidential republic. Rather, the court was concerned that under the new constitution the parliament (the Supreme Kenges) would not have the power to approve the appointments of the prime minister and other members of the cabinet; instead the Supreme Kenges would only "discuss the candidacies." In addition, while parliament can give the government a vote of no confidence, there was a provision specifying that the parliament would be dissolved if there is a vote of no confidence in the government. This provision made it unlikely that any parliament would take such a vote.[40] The new constitution would allow Nazarbayev to have more indirect control over the parliament and over his government and thus be able to proceed with economic reforms in the manner that he wished. The 1995 Constitution of Kazakhstan, under Article 44, section 3 gives the president the right to: "Appoint a Prime Minister of the Republic with the Parliament's consent; release him from office; determine the structure of the Government of the Republic at the proposal of the Prime Minister, appoint to and relieve from office the members thereof."[41]

The new constitution was passed by referendum on August 30, 1995, with some 89 percent of the electorate voting in favor and 90 percent of all voters casting ballots.[42] The new constitution outlined a smaller two-chamber structure of parliament with forty-seven deputies in the upper chamber, the Senate (seven of them appointed by the president) and 55 deputies in the Majlis, the lower chamber, for a total of 102.[43] Recall that the previous two parliaments had 360 deputies (1993) and 177 (1994); fewer politicians to deal with meant fewer problems for the president.

The economic disagreements between Nazarbayev's government and the various parliaments centered on the pace and extent of reform policies. Numerous laws implemented during Nazarbayev's rule by presidential decree greatly advanced the reform program. The Kazakh ambassador to Moscow noted that Nazarbayev had been able to produce more than fifty laws during the three months after the parliament had been dissolved, while during the last year of the 1994 parliament, it had only passed seven.[44] The main areas of legislation implemented during this period are compiled in table 8.

In response to progress in the areas shown in the table along with the country's economic reform program envisioned for 1996–98, the IMF approved a three-year Extended Fund Facility (EFF) for Kazakhstan in July 1996. This type of facility is designed to allow a country to focus on structural reforms, while the Stand-by Arrangement (provided to Kazakhstan in January 1994) is designed to assist with stabilization policies. Thus, the specific order of the lending arrangements from the IMF and the dates that those arrangements were concluded with Kazakhstan and Uzbekistan are indicative of differences in their progress on economic reforms (Fischer 1997). Recall that Uzbekistan had its only SBA from the IMF (provided in December 1995) suspended in March 1997 and that the country had never concluded an agreement for an EFF. A condition of Kazakhstan's acceptance of the EFF from the IMF was that it agreed to end any restricting of current account

## TABLE 8. SIGNIFICANT LEGISLATION DECREED AFTER THE DISBANDING OF THE MARCH 1995 PARLIAMENT

| DATE | LEGISLATION | DESCRIPTION |
| --- | --- | --- |
| April 1995 | Establishment of a Rehabilitation Bank* | Bank would control the financial transactions of enterprises with a large debt burden, with a plan to restructure them. Bank would operate independently from the state under the direction of a board although it would be funded from the state budget. |
| April 1995 | Bankruptcy Law | Included provision for out-of-court settlement; will influence progress of Rehabilitation Bank. |
| June 1995 | Compulsory Medical | Provided universal medical Insurance Fund coverage. Effective January 1996. |
| July 1995 | Revised Budget | Superseded the budget passed by parliament in March 1995. This budget kept the previous deficit target for the year but revised revenue and expenditure expectations based on the new tax code. |
| July 1995 | Tax Code | Simplified and modernized the tax system; the number of taxes was reduced from 49 to 11; representative of systematic laws adhering to international standards. |
| August 1995** | Banking Legislation | Separate investment banks from deposit-taking banks. The idea was to first establish proper accounting methods and then to liberalize the activities of banks. |

* Coordinated with the World Bank.
** In August 1995 the 50 percent surrender requirement for export proceeds was abolished.
sources: IMF 1995, 21; IMF 1996, 17, 23, 27; EBRD 1995, 45–46; EBRD 1996, 156–57; EBRD 1997, 177.

transactions and to avoid discriminatory currency arrangements.[45] The IMF press release documenting the approval of the EFF noted:

> 1995 was the most successful year for the Kazakh economy since independence. Under the authorities' program, supported by a stand-by credit from the IMF, inflation was reduced significantly, and the balance of payments performed consistently better than expected. Progress was made in privatization and public enterprise restructuring and the decline in output began to level off.[46]

Specific progress in small-scale privatization policies included the sale of roughly 70 percent of total eligible firms (those with less than 200 employees) by early 1996. The privatization of large enterprises concentrated in the power, energy, and communications sectors continued through 1997 and resulted in "considerable foreign investment" (EBRD 1997, 176). In 1999, the World Bank published a study comparing the privatization of the power and natural gas industries in Kazakhstan and Hungary, noting that Kazakhstan had made "considerable progress in privatizing its economy." The study also noted that, using the share of GDP accounted for by the private sector (about 60 percent) as a measure, Kazakhstan was ahead of all of the FSU countries, and further, that only in Poland, Hungary, and the Czech Republic (the "advanced reformers") did the private sector account for a greater share of GDP (World Bank 1999, 130). Finally, during 1995, the government also eliminated the state-mandated system for grain and introduced a market-determined system, which included the elimination of administered prices in the agricultural sector (IMF 1996, 19).

Kazakhstan has implemented some of the broadest reforms of all of the Central Asian states. The acceptance of Article VIII obligations and the decision to agree to complete convertibility of the currency was cited by IMF economists as one of the most important steps for the economic reform process in Kazakhstan.[47] Many of these broad reforms were implemented during presidential rule and without the participation of the noncompliant parliaments and other governmental officials who had blocked market reform measures. Nazarbayev has used his presidential authority to bring in a new elite group and one that supports his economic reforms. This transformation is nicely summed up by Martha Brill Olcott (1997, 224) as follows: "An undeniable, if less broadcast, dimension of the deputies' opposition to economic reform has been that privatization (has) shift(ed) economic advantage away from the Soviet-era elite, the nomenklatura, to a new elite."

No members of the early Kazakh government remained as government officials into the mid-1990s. Additionally, the fact that no members from the early 1992 Kazakh government continued in the government as of 2008, is a strong indicator of the high turnover of the former Soviet elite. It should be noted that, in a pattern similar to that involving the Uzbek governmental officials, Nazarbayev did keep in power persons whom he trusted. This practice can be seen in the reappointment of officials from the failed Tereschenko government to the Kazhegeldin government and in the continuation of Vladimir Shkolnik from the Tereschenko government into subsequent governments with his last position as minister of industry and trade in the 2009 administration.[48]

## The Two Presidents and Their Elite

There are two fundamental differences between the economic reform paths and governing styles of Presidents Karimov and Nazarbayev. Karimov advocated the delay of economic reform and orchestrated a relatively low turnover of the former Soviet elite. Nazarbayev wanted to move quickly on reform policies and, in order to do so, had to force a high turnover of the former elite. Thus, diverging views that the two men held on economic reform determined their divergent actions toward their former elite. These actions explain the current support base for the president and the composition of the elite in both countries. Karimov's support comes from people who benefit from economic distortions, while Nazarbayev's support comes from people who benefit from economic reforms.[49] The elite themselves certainly matter, but they have to be understood in the context of their support, or lack thereof, for the president's policies, in addition to the context in which the president's policies were shaped. Chapter 1 of this volume provided the context for the latter part of the analysis, while the previous chapter and this chapter provided the necessary information about each president in order to present a comprehensive analysis of economic and political reform.

## The Future of Reform

The beginning part of this section on the future prospects for reform will briefly discuss the political changes that have occurred in the Kazakhstan; the second part will focus on the economic progress.

### POLITICAL REFORM

Elections for the parliament were held in December 1995; on December 5 for the upper chamber, the Senate, and on December 9 for the lower chamber, the Majlis. Nazarbayev expressed his "deep satisfaction" with the first round of elections and the manner in which they were conducted.[50] Indeed, Nazarbayev had a much more cordial relationship with this parliament, although he continued to go through prime ministers. Kazhegeldin lasted only until 1997, to be followed by Nurlan Balgimbayev, Kasymzhomart Tokayev, and Daniyal Adhmetov. Karim Massimov has been prime minister since 2007. Thus, Nazarbayev has had occasional fallings out with his prime ministers involving differences over economic reform, or his concern over their future political ambitions. For example, it appeared that Kazhegeldin was possibly benefiting too much from his contacts with foreign investors and Western business interests, and there was speculation that he had higher political ambitions, including a run in the presidential elections scheduled for December 2000. Nazarbayev's compliant parliament "unexpectedly" announced in October 1998 that the presidential elections would be moved up to January 1999, and on November 4, 1998, Kazhegeldin was banned from running because of his participation in an unregistered organization, thereby eliminating the only serious opposition to Nazarbayev.[51] The OSCE, which did send observers to monitor the elections, refused to recognize the results, arguing that they were undemocratic (Freedom House 1999–2000, 264).

The next presidential elections were held in Kazakhstan in December 2005, and while Nazarbayev was the "clear winner," garnering 91 percent of the vote, the election "did not meet a number of OSCE commitments and other international standards for democratic elections."[52] Nazarbayev was popular, and it is likely he would have won without any governmental interference, but with a smaller percentage of the vote. In a final twist to the interesting saga of Nazarbayev and his many parliaments, on May 18, 2007, the parliament voted "overwhelmingly" to change the constitution to exempt Nazarbayev from the limit on consecutive presidential terms. This amendment was granted to Nazarbayev because of his "historic role in the formation of [the] state."[53] Certainly, Nazarbayev has played an historic role in facilitating the economic transition of Kazakhstan.

### ECONOMIC REFORM

As I have discussed previously, one of the most important economic reforms that Kazakhstan implemented was currency convertibility in 1996. Kazakhstan's EBRD rating in its trade and foreign exchange system was the highest in 1996, following the reforms implemented in 1995 (see table 6). Again, this is a very different situation from that seen in Uzbekistan, in that even though the latter agreed to currency convertibility in 2003, its rating did not increase until 2005, and even then it increased only marginally (see table 5).

In a sign of the continuing Russian influence over Kazakhstan, decreases in the EBRD indicator in 1999 likely had to do with the devaluation of the Russian ruble in 1998. This policy resulted in substantial financial problems for Kazakhstan, including the depreciation of its currency and an increase in inflation (Gürgen 2000). Kazakhstan trades heavily with Russia, and Russian demand for Kazakhstan's exports decreased following devaluation of the ruble (Olcott 2002, 133–34). While Russia enacted trade restrictions at the beginning of the devaluation crisis, they were eliminated by the end of March 2000 (EBRD 2001a, 12).

The government of Kazakhstan has been commended for its successful macroeconomic achievements since 2000, including halving the unemployment rate and tripling per capita income. Although rural poverty is still high, the country's overall poverty rate has decreased from 30 percent in 2001 to 20 percent in 2003 to 18 percent in 2006.[54] While these accomplishments are due to responsible macroeconomic policies, high oil prices and easy global liquidity have also been factors in the country's economic improvement (Husain 2007).

Indeed, there has been renewed attention to large oil and natural gas resources as a potential economic "curse":[55] many countries that rely heavily on the export of such commodities, especially oil, become dependent on the revenue derived from their export and do not diversify their economies. This curse has struck Kazakhstan, since construction, transportation, and processing related to oil extraction accounted for 16.6 percent of GDP in 2005, while fuel and oil products comprised 69 percent of exports. Meanwhile, the share of manufacturing as a percentage of exports in 2005 fell to less than half the level in 1999 (World Bank 2006).

The other component of the curse, referred to as "Dutch disease," has to do with rising inflation caused by surpluses of foreign currency. Kazakhstan has enacted measures to guard against this danger by creating the National Fund of the Republic of Kazakhstan (NFRK), an oil stabilization fund established in 2000. This fund is designed to control inflation and to mitigate future balance-of-payments problems (when the price of oil goes down). It has been noted by the IMF as a positive step in avoiding "Dutch disease" (IMF 2003b). Kazakh authorities have used the resources from this fund to cushion shocks to the economy during the current economic downturn. The Kazakh government decided to use $5 billion (out of an estimated $25 billion) of the NFRK in order to stabilize the economic situation.[56]

The economic crisis that befell the developed countries in 2008 is likely to affect Kazakhstan more than Uzbekistan because the former is more integrated into the international economy; indeed, Kazakhstan will be more affected by the economic downturn than Russia. This integration is most evident in the banking sector. The Kazakh government dealt with problems in the banking sector by purchasing problem assets of banks and by buying stakes of up to 25 percent in the country's four largest banks in November 2008.[57] This step was necessary because Kazakh banks were dependent on external financing, which helped support domestic credit growth and lending to the household, trade, and construction sectors. Like the banking sectors in most countries, as a result of substantially decreased liquidity, banks are not lending, resulting in declines in property prices and a general slowing of the economy (IMF 2008b, 3–4).

In an hour-long television interview, Nazarbayev explained the economic problems facing his country and asserted that it had the economic resources to get through the crisis.[58] He noted that money had been provided to alleviate problems in the construction sector, and that pension and public-sector salaries would increase in 2009 and 2010. In addition he stated that the government would guarantee bank deposits of up to 5 million tenge (about $40,000) in order to avoid a run on the banks. Finally, in a sign that Nazarbayev still holds his government and in particular his prime minister responsible for economic progress, during an October 2008 cabinet session he told Massimov, "It is time you banged your fist on the table and started working normally," adding that during this time period the government had "carte blanche to carry out a program to stabilize the economy and financial system, and wide powers to make non-standard decisions."[59]

While the financial crisis and economic downturn certainly present challenges for Kazakhstan, it is important to note that the country does have the financial resources and technical expertise to deal with the situation. This is in large part due to Nazarbayev's persistence in shaping the country's economic reform as he had envisioned it. Kazakhstan's program to fix the country's banking sector was praised by an IMF official, and the Kazakh government hired consultants from Credit Suisse and J.P. Morgan to oversee the bailout plan.[60] The following chapter will analyze the divergence in economic reform policies implemented by Kazakhstan and Uzbekistan in such areas as foreign investment legislation, tax legislation, and banking reform and will link these differences to the resulting levels of investment and business in the two countries.

# 4

# Connecting Specific Reform Policies to Investment and Business

The previous chapters provided explanations for differences between the reform policies of Kazakhstan and Uzbekistan. This chapter expands upon this analysis by examining how the implementation of reform policies has influenced foreign investment and business decisions in the two countries. Interviews conducted with representatives of U.S. firms that had either invested in or conducted business in the countries confirmed a relationship between higher levels of investment and business and Kazakhstan's advanced economic reforms in areas such as foreign investment legislation, tax legislation, and banking system reform. Uzbekistan's lack of progress in these areas has affected the level of investment in the country but has had a smaller impact on the number of firms conducting business, which was an unexpected finding. The results of the interviews show that while firms involved in business transactions in both countries secured financing for their business through an export credit agency—the U.S. Export-Import Bank—the use of this bank was a more crucial part of conducting business in Uzbekistan. This was because firms, in effect, mitigated their risks of conducting business there by using the U.S. Export-Import Bank.

## Investment and Economic Reform

It was widely understood that economic reform would be necessary early in the transition process to encourage foreign investment in the transition economies.

## TABLE 9. NET FDI INFLOWS IN THE FORMER SOVIET UNION SUCCESSOR STATES (MILLIONS OF US$)

| | RESOURCE RANK | 1994 | 1996 | 1998 | 2000 | 2002 | 2004 | 2006 | 2008 (EST.) |
|---|---|---|---|---|---|---|---|---|---|
| Armenia | poor | 8 | 18 | 221 | 104 | 111 | 217 | 340 | 482 |
| Azerbaijan | rich | 22 | 661 | 1,024 | 149 | 1,048 | 2,351 | −1,301 | −555 |
| Belarus | poor | 11 | 105 | 201 | 119 | 453 | 163 | 351 | 2,143 |
| Georgia | moderate | 8 | 54 | 221 | 153 | 122 | 420 | 1,115 | 1,177 |
| Kazakhstan | rich | 635 | 1,137 | 1,136 | 1,278 | 2,164 | 5,436 | 6,663 | 10,732 |
| Kyrgyzstan | poor | 38 | 47 | 109 | −7 | 5 | 132 | 182 | 265 |
| Moldova | poor | 18 | 23 | 88 | 127 | 132 | 146 | 223 | 679 |
| Russia | rich | 500 | 1,665 | 1,734 | −463 | −72 | 1,662 | 10,753 | 20,000 |
| Tajikistan | poor | 12 | 18 | 25 | 24 | 36 | 272 | 66 | 190 |
| Turkmenistan | rich | 103 | 108 | 62 | 131 | 276 | 354 | 731 | 820 |
| Ukraine | moderate | 151 | 531 | 744 | 594 | 698 | 1,711 | 5,737 | 9,683 |
| Uzbekistan | moderate | 73 | 90 | 140 | 75 | 65 | 177 | 174 | 755 |

SOURCES: IMF 2000b, 115 (source for resource ranking); EBRD 2001c, 68; EBRD 2009.

Therefore, economists and others advocated reforms aimed at creating a favorable investment climate as a necessary precursor for foreign investment (Fischer and Gelb 1991). Indeed, many studies have shown an important relationship between, on one hand, progress in areas such as political and economic stability and the establishment of a legal and regulatory framework, and on the other, increased foreign investment in the advanced reformers of the Central and Eastern European states and the Baltics (see, e.g., Meyer 1998; Michalet 1997; Bevan and Estrin 2004). Research on foreign direct investment (FDI) into the former Soviet Union states has not been as extensive, primarily because of the comparatively small amounts of investment in these countries and the concentration of early investments in the natural resource sectors (Meyer and Pind 1999). Indeed, the resource-rich former Soviet states (Azerbaijan, Kazakhstan, Russia, and Turkmenistan) generally received higher investment amounts than the other FSU states during the middle to late 1990s, as depicted in table 9.

The foreign investment in these countries has been concentrated in the oil and gas sectors. In Kazakhstan, this sector had the largest share of foreign investment for the years 1993–96 and each individual year thereafter through 2001 (IMF 2002, 99; 2003a, 104). With its reserves of petroleum, natural gas, and gold, Uzbekistan has moderate natural resources according to the IMF rankings

TABLE 10. CUMULATIVE FDI INFLOWS IN THE FORMER SOVIET UNION SUCCESSOR STATES AND
NATURAL RESOURCE ENDOWMENT RANKING

|  | NATURAL RESOURCE RANKING | CUMULATIVE FDI INFLOWS 1989–2008 (MILLIONS OF US$) |
|---|---|---|
| Armenia | poor | 2,599 |
| Azerbaijan | rich | 3,229 |
| Belarus | poor | 6,708 |
| Georgia | moderate | 6,054 |
| Kazakhstan | rich | 48,433 |
| Kyrgyzstan | poor | 1,226 |
| Moldova | poor | 2,442 |
| Russia | rich | 45,045 |
| Tajikistan | poor | 965 |
| Turkmenistan | rich | 4,748 |
| Ukraine | moderate | 40,753 |
| Uzbekistan | moderate | 2,889 |

SOURCES: IMF 2000b, 115; EBRD 2009.

(IMF 2000b, 115). Yet Uzbekistan has received markedly less investment than Ukraine and Georgia, also countries with moderate resources. In fact, data on cumulative investment in the former Soviet states for the period 1989–2008 indicate that a country's endowment in natural resources is only part of the explanation for high or low amounts of investment (see table 10).

For example, Turkmenistan and Azerbaijan had less FDI than three non-resource-rich countries (Ukraine, Belarus, and Georgia). An early study on the transition economies surveyed firms that either planned or had undertaken investment projects in the CEE and former Soviet states and found that progress in transition and that low perceived risks were associated with FDI amounts (Lankes and Venables 1996). Thus, much of the variation in FDI in these countries can be explained by the risk that investors believe that they engage in by doing business or investing in these countries. Investors try to mitigate their risks of investment, and one important way they do so is to determine the likelihood that the host government will honor the contract with the firm. Therefore, firms consider a country's progress toward a market economy, in addition to the type of risk undertaken in an investment or business decision.

Business risks generally carry lower costs than investment risks, especially ones that involve natural resource infrastructure. This relative cost explains in part why Belarus had such high cumulative investment levels. Its authoritarian government structure is seen as a stable entity that reduces the risks for a firm's investment in sectors other than natural resources. Belarus was often (surprisingly) ranked with other advanced transition economies on the quality of governance and security of property rights issues in surveys of business firms conducted during 1999 and 2002. Firms generally did not view the state as an obstacle to their business, "since it continues to perform many of the functions that it carried out under the old regime in an economy that still has strong resemblance to the previous system" (EBRD 1999, 117). States engaged in partial reforms were problematic because they were unable to provide some protections and services during the transition to a market-based system. Finally, the advanced reformers were ranked high on governance and property rights since they had made the most progress in removing the state's control over the economy (EBRD 1999, 116–17). Investments in the natural resource sectors of the former Soviet countries, however, carry a higher level of risk because they rely on a willingness of the government to follow the legal procedures and to enforce the contracts that are required in a market economy.

Theodore Moran's (1999; 2006) research on investment in natural resources in the developing and transition economies finds that these countries pose unique challenges for investors because there are more risks involved in long-term projects, including nationalistic actions on the part of the host government, which most often occur in the mining and petroleum sectors. Petroleum exploration in particular poses economic and political risks, including the potential for change in tax structures and foreign-exchange remittance restrictions (van Meurs 1971; Moran 1998; 1981). Jonathan Stern (1995) examined the important economic and political issues that Western corporations would consider in their decisions on investment in Russia and the CIS to develop natural resources.[1] He categorized them as a "short-list of the most important issues" (1995, 59):

- Central/regional/local political relationships
- Political stability at national, regional and local levels
- Implementation and stability of legal and fiscal frameworks
- Low domestic prices and nonpayment problems, combined with nonconvertibility of currencies.

Indeed, Pomfret (2006, 154) has noted that one of the reasons that large oil firms decided not to continue with exploration of oil fields in Turkmenistan was "difficulties in dealing with the regime." In addition, while Kazakhstan and

Russia are both rich in natural resources, predominately in the oil and gas sectors, Kazakhstan received larger cumulative FDI amounts for the period 1989–2008 than did Russia (see table 10). This is somewhat surprising because Russia has the largest natural gas reserves and the eighth largest oil reserves in the world, and has its own pipeline systems to export its oil. However, Russia's state-owned oil and gas companies have been working to obtain controlling stakes in projects that were previously foreign owned, leading foreign firms to believe that the risks of doing business in the country may be too great.

Studies that have surveyed investors and business representatives provide additional information on progress toward a market economy and risk indicators and were used in part to develop the framework for my analysis of the investment climate in Kazakhstan and Uzbekistan. One study that surveyed investors and IMF staff on factors that influenced a country's investment climate concluded that investment is hindered by corruption, weak legal frameworks, difficult tax systems, and incomplete structural reforms in the banking, civil service, and energy sectors (Shiells 2003). Some of the most comprehensive assessments of the business and investment climate in the transition economies were the Business Environment and Enterprise Performance Surveys (BEEPS) undertaken in 1999 and 2002 jointly by the EBRD and the World Bank (EBRD 1999, 2002). These surveys questioned managers of enterprises in the region on the investment climate, focusing on improvement in macroeconomic conditions (including exchange rate and policy stability) and asking managers to rank "broader investment climate" issues such as taxation, the judiciary, law and order, and finance and infrastructure services as obstacles to the firm's investment or business (EBRD 1999, 40, 139–40).

Since investors are concerned about the security of their investments and the possibility of changes in contracts once projects are under way, they are interested in contractual and investment-related aspects of reform when considering investment and business in the natural resource sector (Johnston 1994; Stern 1995). Improvements in the investment climate need to include an equitable, efficient, and transparent tax regime and a stable legal and regulatory climate.[2] This chapter, which identifies the specific areas of reform deemed important in investing and conducting business in Kazakhstan and Uzbekistan, builds upon the areas targeted by previous studies. The results of the interviews reported here indicate that in their investment and business decisions representatives focus on trade and foreign exchange liberalization; legal and structural reforms, including a modern tax system; foreign investment legislation; and banking sector reform.

## Interviews with Investor and Business Representatives

Interviews with investor and business representatives were conducted to determine the specific economic reforms that they consider important factors in their investment and business decisions in Kazakhstan and Uzbekistan. I hypothesized that there would be a positive correlation between economic reforms and levels of investment and business, with Kazakhstan's advanced economic reforms resulting in greater investment, and Uzbekistan's lack of progress on reform leading to lower levels of investment and business. In other words, the success of economic reforms explains levels of foreign investment and business. The interviews also shed light on the relationship between economic reforms and investment in natural resources. This is important because some studies have found that a country with large exportable primary commodities may delay reform because of the large inflows of capital from those exports, an outcome known as the "resource curse."[3] The hypothesis is that states that are rich in natural resources usually delay reforms, engage in rent-seeking, and have slow economic growth because the government does not diversify the economy, relying on revenue from the export of those commodities. Terry Lynn Karl's (1997, 190) study theorizes that oil-producing countries often become "rentier state" regimes with weak and unaccountable state institutions, a type of regime that is unlikely to institute sound economic policy.

Erika Weinthal and Pauline Jones Luong (2001) take an alternative approach in analyzing whether the resource curse is operative in the energy-rich former Soviet states.[4] They examine differences in the privatization processes of these states and conclude that the curse is more likely to occur when the resources are state owned instead of privatized, and further, that the privatization process should be carried out by domestic actors (as was the case in Russia) rather than foreign investors (as was the case in Kazakhstan) to create a viable tax regime.[5] I extend their analysis by examining whether there is a correlation between the *specific* reforms undertaken during the transition process as a necessary component of foreign investment. Recall that Kazakhstan was intimately connected with Russia during the Soviet era, and for many reasons needed to better integrate itself with the international community in order to succeed as an independent state. The country also lacked the infrastructure needed to benefit from the export of its commodities without foreign assistance. This is a situation very different from that in Uzbekistan, and is one reason that the country moved more slowly on reform policies. These differences were also noted by EBRD economists in explaining possible factors in the different reform strategies followed by the energy-rich states:

> There are important differences within the energy-rich countries. On the one hand, Kazakhstan and Russia are among the most advanced reformers in the CIS, despite having backtracked temporarily on external liberalization after the Russian crisis in 1998. Since then, governments in both countries seem to have adopted a cautious yet positive approach to liberalization. Azerbaijan, in spite of shortcomings in institutional reforms and governance, has maintained a liberal external trade regime and used oil revenues carefully for budget and current account financing. Turkmenistan and Uzbekistan, on the other hand, have failed to make or maintain reform progress. Both Turkmenistan and Uzbekistan had access to early income from gas, cotton and gold exports, whereas in Azerbaijan and Kazakhstan potential energy rents had to be unlocked by attracting foreign investment. This might explain the different paths of reform in these countries. (EBRD 2001c, 80)

What "unlocked" the foreign investment in the country? Was it Kazakhstan's reforms? Or, as some have asserted, are reforms less important when a country has large resource reserves such as oil?[6] Which areas of economic reform matter the most for FDI and business? This chapter will answer these questions by examining the links between reforms implemented by each country and the corresponding volume and type of investment and business deemed important by U.S. investor and business representatives.[7]

## Characteristics of Firms

U.S. firms were contacted for interviews since the United States provides the largest share of investment in Kazakhstan, and U.S. firms are significant investors in Uzbekistan.[8] Areas of investment and business in the two countries have included oil and gas, gold, agriculture, minerals, aerospace, telecommunications, and consumer goods.[9] I therefore contacted enterprises involved in those sectors and interviewed representatives from them.[10] Personal interviews were chosen for this study in order to gather information about each respondent's interpretation of the impacts of reform on investment and business decisions.[11] Anonymity was granted to the respondents; I also received requests that the name of the firm not be given. Thus, I categorized firms in the following way: those that made direct investment in natural resources (natural resource firms); those that contracted

| TABLE 11. STANDARD INDUSTRIAL CLASSIFICATIONS (*SIC*) OF SURVEYED FIRMS | | | |
| --- | --- | --- | --- |
| SIC | NATURAL RESOURCE | SERVICE | BUSINESS |
| | Crude Petroleum<br>Natural Gas | Oil, Gas Field<br>Machinery/Equipment | Radio/Telecommunication<br>Equipment |
| | Crude Petroleum<br>Natural Gas | Engineering Services | Farm Machinery/Equipment |
| | Petroleum Refining | Construction/Engineering | Aircraft |
| | Petroleum Refining | Oil, Gas Field Services | Construction/<br>Machinery Equipment |
| | | | Aircraft |
| | Gold Ores | | Soap/Detergent* |
| | | | Steam, Gas,<br>Hydraulic Turbines** |
| | | | Cigarettes |
| | | | Farm Machinery/Equipment |
| *N* | 5 | 4 | 9 |
| Avg. Sales (US$ millions) | 176,000 | 11,600*** | 53,653 |
| Avg. No. of Employees | 59,000 | 53,000*** | 120,002 |

*Except specialty cleaners.
**And turbine generator set units.
***One of the four service firms is privately owned and comparative data on sales and number of employees was not available.
SOURCE: Dow Jones Business Interactive LLC (trading as Factiva). Accessed December 21, 2005.

with a natural resource firm (service firms); and those that did business with the government of the country or private firms (business firms). Specific information about the firms, including their Standard Industrial Classification (SIC), their size (represented by average sales and average number of employees), and the number of firms interviewed in each category, is provided in table 11.

The following sections describe how each type of firm (natural resource, service, or business) discerned the importance of economic reform in the firm's specific investment or business decisions. The data shows that this categorization illustrates differences in the degree and types of economic reforms that representatives considered to be important in their decisions.

### NATURAL RESOURCE FIRMS

The results in table 12 indicate a number of trends in firms' investment in development of natural resources. First, although questions (2) and (9) may seem likely to elicit the same answer—with the responses to question (9) providing

## TABLE 12. RESULTS OF QUESTIONNAIRE, NATURAL RESOURCE FIRMS (*N* = 5)

| QUESTION | YES | NO | OTHER |
|---|---|---|---|
| **2.** Did the *country's* implementation of economic reform influence the investment decision? | 1 | 4 | |
| **3.** In Kazakhstan/Uzbekistan were there any individuals or ministry heads that representatives were required to meet with, or that in meeting with them, any problems were more easily solved? | 5 | | |
| If yes, do you feel comfortable stating which ministers? | 4 | | 1 |
| **4.** Does the firm use country risk assessments? | 5 | | |
| **8.** Does the value of the natural resource override an analysis of economic reform in the country? | 1 | 2 | 1—yes and no<br>1—if the risk is big, can we receive a larger payment? |
| **9.** Was there an *aspect* of economic reform that influenced the investment decision? | 4 | 1 | |
| If yes, what was it?<br>Contract law; upholding contracts<br>Production Sharing Agreements (PSAs)<br>Sanctity of contract (2 representatives) | | | |

NOTE: I used one questionnaire for interviews with representatives of natural resource firms. I did not use a separate questionnaire for representatives with investment in Kazakhstan and then a separate questionnaire for representatives with investment in Uzbekistan. I combined some of the questions, replacing Kazakhstan and Uzbekistan with the phrase 'the country' in order to avoid repetition in the table.

more detail—the representatives interpreted the two questions differently.[12] A business associate familiar with business and investment, primarily in Uzbekistan, offered this opinion on their reasoning: "Representatives likely define economic reform as the overall macroeconomic reform process. They view this term as indicative of the governments' overall strategy of reform, and thus the representatives think that you are asking if the broad overall economic political reform was important."[13] The associate also commented that "the firm is only interested in the specific areas or sectors that matter to their investment."[14] Thus, the responses suggest that reform in general is not critical, just reform in areas that affect the firm's activity. The only representative to answer question (2) in the affirmative gave the following explanation: "Kazakhstan was one of the first and way ahead of the rest of the other countries to bring in advisors, technical assistance to help with their foreign investment laws; the tax laws enacted were very far ahead of other countries."[15] This representative explained that an agreement that the firm had signed with the country looked at tax law and the overall investment climate to make sure that the investment would not be nationalized.[16] It appears that this representative understood question (2) as a correlate with question (9).

Question (8), "Does the value of the natural resource override an analysis of economic reform in the country?" elicits a mixed response. The question was designed to find out whether firms are willing to overlook the potential for investment-related problems in the natural resource sector, generally oil production. One of the representatives who responded no to the question explained that his or her firm "does not just go anywhere" (the firm was not in Nigeria or Yemen, for example) and that "the level of taxation and tax regime issues were very important."[17] The representative stated that the size of the risk was a factor: "If the risk is so high, the firm is concerned about losing investment," but "when we are discussing billions of barrels of oil, you try to ameliorate the risk, try to work it out."[18]

Two representatives of natural resource firms stated that they had looked into investing in Uzbekistan for production of natural gas; both in the end decided against the investment. One firm was concerned about the small reserves of gas and its use primarily for domestic purposes. The firm conducted exploration in the country and believed there was potential in the sector.[19] However, the representative explained that for the firm's purposes, Uzbekistan had small resources and that "gas is not attractive if it is used internally, because it wouldn't be as profitable. Someone has to pay [the investing firm], whether it is the country or the Uzbek citizens, but they [investors] want it to be the most profitable situation."[20] Thus, Uzbekistan's use of the gas primarily for domestic purposes and the government's ongoing subsidies for gas (see chapter 1) had affected the firm's investment decision.

The other firm seemed to be convinced by investment-related problems. Its representative stated that the firm "probably" looked at the gas sector in Uzbekistan but "ran away." When I asked whether the firm considered Kazakhstan a more stable environment for the firm's investment than Uzbekistan, the representative responded, "Actions speak louder than words"; the firm had investment in Kazakhstan.[21] These responses indicate that the broader investment climate influenced the decision of the firm not to pursue investment in Uzbekistan.

It is also important to note that the only representative who answered definitively that the value of the natural resource overrode an analysis of economic reform in the country was the same one who answered that there were no aspects of economic reform that influenced investment in the country (see questions (8) and (9) in table 12). At one time this representative's firm had invested in both Kazakhstan and Uzbekistan, but the "project in Kazakhstan had been concluded" only because "it was not profitable enough" and "issues of reform had nothing to do with it."[22] This representative elaborated on the areas that were important to the firm:

> The natural resource does override an analysis of economic reform, but the project agreed on is important. Economic risk is mitigated by negotiating an arrangement with the government. Economic reform is good [privatization of the sector assets] but more importantly the firm wants assurances that the agreement will be upheld. [The firm] has a partnership with the government including a specific tax decree that is specific to the firm.[23]

Therefore, while natural resource firms do consider aspects, or sector-specific areas, of reform, the areas of concern are directly related to the sector of the investment. The aforementioned representative stated that political stability in the country was more important than economic reform; the example provided was that the firm had investment in Ghana and that Karimov was considered stable. Additionally, when this representative answered question (3) about meeting with governmental officials, he or she stated that "meeting with the president [Karimov] and prime ministers was essential and was fundamental to continuing operations."[24] The importance of meeting with governmental officials may also be seen in the responses of business firm representatives, but not those of service firm representatives.

### SERVICE FIRMS

Service firms as defined in this study are those that have engaged in engineering, construction, and project management in the oil and gas fields in Kazakhstan or Uzbekistan. At the outset of the interview process, the service firms were not separated from the firms with direct investment. Primarily this was because I presumed that they would have the same considerations as the firms with direct investment. After I conducted interviews with representatives from these firms and followed up with questions to clarify their responses, it became clear that these firms had different assessments of the importance of economic reform than did direct-investing firms.

This distinction became evident when all four representatives of service firms whom I interviewed told me that neither economic reform nor the value of the natural resource influenced their decisions. Instead they "go where their client [the direct-investing firm] goes" (three representatives) and go to these countries "if the big firms are there" (one representative). In short, the representatives stated that their risk and, therefore, their focus on economic reform in a sector was minimal because their contracts were arranged with the direct-investing firms, not with the countries. In effect, they had a very different assessment of risk that was affected (they presumed) by the behavior of bigger firms that would not be there if the risk were too great. Specific reasons given for their differing assessment of risk included a shorter time horizon of three to four years for their firm's involvement, as opposed to ten-plus years of involvement for the direct-investing firms. The representatives explained that economic reforms were not a consideration for the following reasons:

- These firms assume that the bigger firms would not be in a country in the first place if there were serious risks involved.
- The bigger firms would deal with those issues; thus there was more of an emphasis on where the client (the direct-investing firm) goes.
- The contracts with the direct-investing firms stipulated that the service firms would get paid immediately, often before the contract would begin. The only risk would be that personnel would have to be relocated.[25]

The services firms were not exposed to the same type of risk as the investing firms, which are exposed to long-term risk, estimated by one representative of a natural resource firm to run between twenty and forty years. In addition, the risk borne by direct investors is of a qualitatively different type, specifically associated with losing sunk capital to nationalization.[26] Instead, the risk for the services firms is largely alleviated through the involvement of the natural resource firms.

The representatives from the natural resource firms, by contrast, were concerned about the economic and political risks posed by their investment decisions; they mitigated this risk by examining reforms implemented in each country, specifically contractual and investment legislation. The areas of economic reform considered most important included foreign investment laws, contract legislation, and Production Sharing Agreements (PSAs) (see table 12).[27] Reasons given for not investing in Uzbekistan included the smaller reserves of the resource and concern about whether Uzbekistan was a stable environment.

Progress in the areas deemed important by the investors' representatives is examined in the following section. Specific comparisons are based on each country's progress in establishing foreign investment legislation, a modern tax system, and enforceable contracts.

## Areas of Investment Legislation

### KAZAKHSTAN

Kazakhstan enacted its first Law on Foreign Investment in December 1994. It defined both legal and economic principles for foreign investment, including the protection of the investment and procedures for settling disputes through arbitration authorities (OECD 1998, 40–43). An important component of this legislation was that foreign investors would be protected from changes in legislation for at least ten years from the time of their investment if the changes in the legislation would disadvantage the foreign investor (OECD 1998, 76). The law additionally provided a framework for settling disputes between the investor and a state body: if a settlement was not reached by negotiation, then the investment dispute could be heard by international arbitration authorities, including the International Centre for the Settlement of Investment Disputes (ICSID) and arbitration authorities established by the United Nations organization for International Trade Law (UNCITRAL) (OECD 1998, 42–43). The arbitration clause was an important component for settling disputes because it outlined the rules and procedures whereby disputes would be settled if a conflict developed. Importantly, Kazakhstan's agreement to international arbitration meant that the dispute would not be heard by local courts, which in many cases would mean that a decision could be influenced by the domestic government (Johnston 1994, 168–69).

The new tax code legislation passed in July 1995 (via presidential decree) was also important for investors because it modernized the tax system, improved incentives for investors by reducing tax rates, and standardized the tax rates (EBRD 1996, 157; also see table 10). For example, the corporate income tax was set at a standard rate of 30 percent, the value-added tax (VAT) was set at a uniform rate of 20 percent, and the number of taxes was reduced from forty-nine to eleven (IMF 1996, appendix 2, secs. 1.2 and 3.1, pp. 55–57). This tax code was in effect until 2002 and "was considered to be among the most comprehensive pieces of tax legislation in the former Soviet Union" (Suhir and Kovach 2003, 4). The legislation did provide for a natural resource tax, but there was no set rate. Instead, the relevant section stated that the tax "varies depending on the contract" (IMF 1996, appendix 2, sec. 5, p. 59). This clause explains why investors in natural resources stated that contracts and contract legislation were important components of their investment decisions.

Kazakhstan was also the first FSU country to pass petroleum legislation, an indication of its emphasis on attracting investment in this sector, which appears to have been Nazarbayev's focus for quite some time (OECD 1998, 115). An important component of this legislation was "On Oil," passed by presidential decree on June 28, 1995. Nazarbayev used his authority to issue this decree based on powers accorded him through the legislation, "On the Temporary Delegation of Additional Powers to the President of the Republic of Kazakhstan and the Heads of Local Administrations," passed on December 10, 1993, when the Supreme Soviet agreed to self-dissolve (see the previous chapter).[28] According to the analysis by Rosemarie Forsythe (1996, 35), the legislation had gone through at least twenty drafts before it was finally passed by presidential decree, but only after the parliament elected in 1994 was disbanded in 1995. It provides additional protections, among them this guarantee to investors: "If commercial amounts are discovered, a prospecting-license holder has the exclusive right to obtain an extraction license on condition that the requirements set down in prospecting-license have been met" (Russia and Eurasia Documents Annual 1995, 290). This section of the legislation was noted in an analysis by the Organization for Economic Cooperation and Development; it was stronger than Russian oil legislation that granted only a "priority right," not an exclusive right (OECD 1998, 117).

PSAs (or contracts) are important because they provide a framework for determining production areas, rights and obligations of contractors, the valuation of petroleum (whether paid in cash under a service contract, or whether the contractor has a crude purchase agreement with the oil company), and arbitration (see Johnston 1994, 156–70). PSAs are often viewed as representative of a country's overall commitment to creating an attractive legal and investment climate. One representative from a natural resource firm stated that the area of economic reform that the firm examined was the "host government's willingness to honor the contract"; as an example, the representative cited Russia's reneging on a PSA as an example of a government not honoring the law.[29]

Representatives' characterizations of Kazakhstan's commitment to its contracts were surprising in light of the country's previous attempts to alter its investment-related legislation. In April 2001, legislation was proposed that would have required the approval of the Kazakh government before a dispute with a foreign investor could be taken before international arbitration, a sharp contrast to the previous investment law passed in 1994.[30] A new tax code was passed in July 2001, retroactive to January 2001, that reduced the VAT rate from 20 percent to 16 percent; however, the VAT in the oil and mining sectors remained at the higher rate unless the firm agreed to negotiate compensatory measures in PSAs and other contracts (EBRD 2001c, 158). In December 2001, President Nazarbayev stressed at a meeting of the Foreign Investors Council that previous contracts would be honored, but that increases in profits from unexpectedly high oil prices should "balance the interests of the state and business."[31]

Apparently since Kazakhstan had altered this tax legislation, a large oil company exercised its option to change its payment structure and move to a faster depreciation schedule because it wanted to renegotiate the tax. The Kazakh government had apparently included as part of its early contract negotiations a provision related to the depreciation of assets. Accelerated depreciation is an accounting method in which assets can be written off at a rate faster than normal "straight line depreciation" and is commonly used to attract investors; accelerated depreciation allows lower tax rates in the early years of a project (Johnston 1994, 293, 302–3). Thus, during 2001, this "major oil company" (the description used in the IMF publication cited) switched to a faster depreciation schedule, resulting in a drop of nearly one percentage point in Kazakhstan's GDP in 2002, according to the IMF (IMF 2003b, 7). The Kazakh government changed the accounting rules to remove accelerated depreciation in 2003, in order to increase the tax burden on the companies.

During an interview, an IMF economist commented that the situation received "a lot of hype," that is, was not recognized as a crucial moment in the development of a reliable climate for investment.[32] In another interview, a business associate speculated that Nazarbayev's actions were the result of domestic pressures, arising from the perception that early deals were favorable to investors at the expense of the state, and that the change in laws affecting depreciation was designed to restore balance.[33] Theodore Moran comments that it is common for the favorable terms negotiated at early stages of a new market economy to become politically insupportable. Governments must therefore decide "how long an initially generous investment structure should last." As an example, Moran (2006, 86) cites Kazakhstan's favorable terms granted to early investors, which became especially chafing when large reserves of oil were later found.

Firms believe that they have to find a way to negotiate with the Kazakh government because of the huge opportunities presented by the country's oil fields and its relative stability (politically and economically) compared to countries like Nigeria, Venezuela, and even Russia. For example, in February 2004 a consortium of oil companies reached an agreement with the government to develop the Kashagan oil field, described as the largest oil discovery in thirty years, with reserves estimated at 13 billion barrels.[34] Even though the Kazakh government had previously discussed altering oil contract legislation, large oil deals were still being made, because there are only so many places in the world with such large reserves.[35] Natural resource firms are willing to take more risks in Kazakhstan than in Uzbekistan because the potential payoff is much greater. However, the Kazakh government also implemented investor-friendly legislation to encourage investment in the country's resources (Jones-Luong and Weinthal 2001). Uzbekistan has not passed equivalent legislation, an important factor in the decisions of investors not to continue negotiations with the Uzbek government.

### UZBEKISTAN

While representatives of the government of Uzbekistan have stated that it encourages and welcomes foreign investment in developing its natural resources, the country has not implemented the same type of framework for investment as Kazakhstan.[36] The main differences between the two countries are in the areas of foreign investment legislation and tax legislation. First, while Uzbekistan passed its first Law on Foreign Investment in May 5, 1994, the law was amended on September 22, 1994, on May 6, 1995, and again on August 30, 1997 (EBRD 1999, 282). Multiple revisions to the legislation make it difficult for investors to keep track of the most recent law and its implications. A new Law on Foreign Investment, passed on April 30, 1998, alleviated some of the previous concerns of investors. For example, Uzbekistan agreed to the ICSID Convention and UNCITRAL for international arbitration, a change from the previous law, and offered some protection to foreign investors. However, in many other areas the legislation did not go far enough to protect investors' rights.

First, investors are concerned about the consequences of changes in legislation because of references in the foreign investment law to guarantees and privileges granted by "current legislation." One problem is that the provisions are subject to other legislation, which either restricts or prohibits the rights of foreign investors.[37] An example is Article 10 of the Law on Foreign Investment, "Rights of Foreign Investors," which provides that investors may:

> independently and freely dispose of income gained as a result of investment activity, and
> use funds in the national currency in their accounts to acquire foreign currency on the domestic currency market.[38]

However, the current legislation passed in 1998 did not allow the convertibility of Uzbek currency (a restriction not changed formally until 2003) and required the conversion of profits into *soum*.[39]

The legislation passed in April 1998 was amended and supplemented in June 14, 1999 and in May 26, 2000.[40] Again, numerous revisions to investment legislation make it difficult for investors to keep track of the most recent changes, and increase concerns that additional changes may be made in the future. According to one business associate, a problem for the Uzbek leadership is that they are trying to attract investment but not necessarily investors: "The leadership wants investors just to be able to send their money. The idea of 'investment' and others making decisions was not a desirable one."[41]

The second major difference in the investment framework in Kazakhstan and Uzbekistan is in the area of tax legislation. Uzbekistan did not pass tax code legislation until January 1998 (Kazakhstan did so in July 1995), and its wording was cumbersome. For example, it provides for an income (profit) tax for most enterprises, but the tax does not have a standard rate, as does Kazakhstan's corporate income tax, and it excludes important enterprises. The excluded enterprises include those in trade and food services, and there are many separate rates, depending on many variables, for production enterprises with foreign investments (see IMF 2000a, appendix 3, no. 1, pp. 95–97). This tax system also provides a "Tax on the Use of Mineral Resources," set at a rate determined by the Cabinet of Ministers. Kazakhstan's tax rate, by contrast, varies by contract. It is likely that investors would be concerned about legislation that permitted the Cabinet of Ministers to arbitrarily change the tax rate, since it could not be established in a contract. In a comparison of hydrocarbon tax structures in transition countries, Uzbekistan made "substantial use" of excise levies for hydrocarbons: 50 percent on oil and 48 percent on gas, as well as other production-based levies. Kazakhstan did not assess either of these levies, and its tax structure provided for a simple profit-based system (EBRD 2001c, table 4.2, p. 83).

### FIRMS WITH BUSINESS INVOLVEMENT

Table 13 categorizes respondents' answers concerning the areas of economic reform that firms considered in their business decisions.

The importance of Export-Import Bank (Ex-Im Bank) financing was not included in the questionnaire; its significance was determined by analysis of the respondents' affirmative answers to question (9), that the aspect of economic reform that had influenced the decision was financing by the U.S. Export-Import Bank.[42] The other aspects of economic reform that influenced business decisions were predictably important factors in business decisions (see the individual responses to question (9) in table 13). The following section explains in more detail the importance of the U.S. Export-Import Bank as an export credit agency (ECA)

## TABLE 13. RESULTS OF QUESTIONNAIRE, BUSINESS FIRMS (*N* = 9)

| QUESTION | YES | NO | OTHER |
|---|---|---|---|
| **2.** Did thecountry's implementation of economic reform influence the investment decision? | 5 | 4 | |
| **3.** In Kazakhstan/Uzbekistan were there any individuals or ministry heads that representatives were required to meet with, or that in meeting with them, any problems that were more easily solved? | 6 | 2 | DNA |
| **4.** Does the firm use country risk assessments? | 6 | 1 | 1—It is influenced by Ex-Im Bank financing.<br>1—The firm is aware of them. |

**9.** Was there an aspect of economic reform that influenced the business decision?

                                                   7      2*

If yes, what was it?

Ex-Im Bank financing . . . . . . . . . . . . . . . . . . . . . . . . . . . . . . . . . . . . . . . . . . . . . . 4

Banking sector development; legal base for commercial activities . . . . . . . . . . 1

Rule of law; freely exchanged currency; repatriation of foreign currency . . . . . 1

Creditworthiness of government; ability to pay . . . . . . . . . . . . . . . . . . . . . . . . . . 1

**17.** Was the Ex-Im Bank used to provide financing for the business?

                                                      5

In Kazakhstan? . . . . . . . . . . . . . . . . . . . . . . . . . . . . . . . . . . . . . . . . . . . . . . . . . . . .1**

In Uzbekistan? . . . . . . . . . . . . . . . . . . . . . . . . . . . . . . . . . . . . . . . . . . . . . . . . . . . . .3

For both? . . . . . . . . . . . . . . . . . . . . . . . . . . . . . . . . . . . . . . . . . . . . . . . . . . . . . . . .1

*This Representative responded, "All we want is to get paid, so we use the Ex-Im Bank." The representative did not relate the aspect of economic reform specifically to Ex-Im Bank financing even though the firm did use the Ex-Im Bank for financing.
**More business in Kazakhstan; less in Uzbekistan because of local production issues.

and how firms use such agencies to mitigate their risks of conducting business with countries that provide uncertain commercial and political environments.

## The U.S. Export-Import Bank

The U.S. Export-Import Bank was created in 1934 by Franklin D. Roosevelt to support exports to international markets by providing financing that was not available through the private sector. Therefore, the bank "does not compete with private sector lenders but provides export financing products that fill gaps in trade financing. [The bank] assume(s) credit and country risks that the private sector is unable or unwilling to accept."[43] The Ex-Im Bank functions more or less as a lender of last resort, although whether it is appropriate for the Bank to function in this manner has been a topic of considerable debate.[44] While the bank assumes some risk that private financing will not, it is expected to lend based on criteria assuring a reasonable expectation of repayment and not to lend below a minimum level of creditworthiness.

The Ex-Im Bank determines a country's creditworthiness and risk and determines whether it will lend (insure financing) on a sovereign (arranged with the state) or nonsovereign (arranged with a private firm) basis.[45] Sovereign lending is the least risky because the government signs a guarantee that the state will use all of its resources to pay the loan; this is referred to as a "sovereign guarantee." Considerations in this type of lending arrangement include the volatility of the political system, the repayment history of the country, its debt burden, its balance of payments, and its macroeconomic performance. Nonsovereign lending is arranged with private firms and carries higher risk. Considerations for this type of lending arrangement include volatility of the political system, vulnerability to a foreign exchange crisis, the country's legal system insofar as it affects banking, available foreign exchange, and the general business climate.[46] The bank provides financing (or is "open") to a country for short-, medium-, or long-term financing and on a sovereign and nonsovereign basis that is determined by economic and political criteria used to assess a country.

The Ex-Im Bank is open to sovereign and nonsovereign lending in Kazakhstan. Kazakhstan was the first of the FSU states to be open across the board in the private sector for short-, medium-, and long-term arrangements. Such decisions by the bank are important because they indicate that it considers the private sector in Kazakhstan to be sufficiently creditworthy that the bank can support financing in that sector. Uzbekistan is only open to sovereign lending for short- and medium-term arrangements.[47] However, Uzbekistan has a perfect repayment record with the bank; it has never defaulted on a loan and therefore has not had to make payments to the bank. Therefore, while Uzbekistan has a lower rating from the bank than Kazakhstan (i.e., only open for sovereign lending in the short or medium term) it is in good standing, so to speak, with the bank.

Kazakhstan has less need for Ex-Im Bank financing because the country can receive commercial financing; it meets the criteria for risk in the private sector.[48] This explains why firms used the Ex-Im Bank less for financing with Kazakhstan. The representative of the lone firm that did use the bank for financing with Kazakhstan did not have the same type of business arrangement with Uzbekistan and stated that the bank was used in Kazakhstan in this instance because of the large amount of business being conducted.[49] Other representatives also stated that more business was done in Kazakhstan because of greater business opportunities.

Three firms used the Ex-Im Bank for business only with Uzbekistan. The reasons that firms used the Ex-Im Bank were that it set up the financing and took the risk if the government did not pay (mentioned by one representative) and that financing by the Ex-Im Bank was crucial to projects going forward (mentioned by two representatives).

The firm that used the Ex-Im Bank for business in both countries has a very interesting situation. The primary reason that the firm had become involved in both countries had to do with upgrading of their airports for use by the U.S. military; the firm was working as a contractor for the U.S. government. The representative stated that "U.S. government interests have become enhanced in the region," as a result of increased coordination on military operations in Afghanistan, although the representative did not explicitly give this explanation. The Export-Import Bank was not needed for those projects because the firm was paid by the U.S. government. Instead the bank was used for "civilian" projects in both countries. Furthermore, the representative stated that the firm "wouldn't be involved in Uzbekistan if the [U.S.] government wasn't there." This is a unique example of "spillover effects," that is, business in one sector of the economy spilling over into other sectors. It is an additional way that the financing structure used by the Ex-Im Bank promotes domestic employment and domestic manufacturing.

The U.S. Export-Import Bank is only permitted to provide financing for 85 percent of an export contract. The firm must pay 15 percent of the contract up front in order for the bank to guarantee financing for the loan. In essence, the bank finances the domestic content of the U.S. export contract and the firm is free to have the 15 percent that it assumes the risk for assembled however it would like. Thus, some of these firms also had manufacturing done in the host countries. The process included the employment of local workers, training programs, and certification of factories for parts assembly. Workers, for example, had assembled parts for a plane in Uzbekistan.[50]

The representatives also stated that developing local industry and employment were important aspects of business deals with the Uzbek government. One representative stated that "the Uzbekistan government viewed it as very important to bring in local manufacturing and local value added" and that the firm "does employ local Uzbeks, probably about five thousand."[51] This aspect of business deals also explains in part the high number (six out of nine) of representatives who stated that meeting with government or ministry heads was either required or helped solve problems (see table 13). This high affirmative response rate was expected for the firms with direct investment in the countries, but the high response rate was surprising for firms only conducting business. Part of the explanation involves the centralized authoritarian structure of both governments. There are few decisions that the president and his respective governmental officials are not involved in; again to quote one of the representatives:

> Absolutely, the chair of [the firm] has a personal relationship with Karimov. You need to have a relationship with the president or the number two or three person. It is a similar situation in Kazakhstan with Nazarbayev. Often in Uzbekistan the minister of agriculture or minister of industry is needed, but more important would be meeting with the minister of finance and the minister of foreign affairs.[52]

Another reason the government is heavily involved in business in Uzbekistan has to do with an emphasis by the its government on creating local employment opportunities; this was mentioned by representatives of three firms as an important component of their business deals in the country. This high level of involvement by the government in creating business opportunities also makes sense in light of the approach that the government has taken with regard to foreign investment in a broader sense. Recall that a business associate stated that, in effect, the Uzbek government did not want others making decisions on its behalf; it wanted to be involved in the decision-making process.[53] Through these business deals, the Uzbek government is able to assert that it is creating jobs for Uzbeks.

Thus, the involvement of the Ex-Im Bank benefited the host country (in this study primarily Uzbekistan) as well as the firm, and to a degree U.S. workers. Although the firm does have to pay 15 percent of the loan for the bank to agree to finance the other 85 percent, representatives stated that as long as the bank was willing to be involved, the risk of possibly losing the 15 percent was outweighed by the benefit for the firm to be able to increase their business. Uzbekistan's demographics as the largest domestic market in Central Asia were an additional factor in the business decisions of these firms.[54]

At the time that these interviews were conducted, Uzbekistan's currency was not convertible, which I hypothesized would affect the decision of firms not to conduct business in the country. However, while the business firms were concerned about currency convertibility, they were able to mitigate the risks associated with nonconvertibility by using the Ex-Im Bank to secure financing for the business. The bank thus alleviated much of the risk that the firms faced by conducting business in Uzbekistan. Therefore, the number of firms conducting business in the country would have been substantially reduced if financing could not be secured through the Ex-Im Bank.

Three representatives mentioned an aspect of economic reform that influenced business decisions and did not have to do with Ex-Im Bank financing (see table 13). One representative of a firm that conducted less business in Uzbekistan than in Kazakhstan stated that areas of economic reform that were important to the firm included banking sector development and a legal base for commercial activities.[55] Another representative of a firm that had conducted business only in Kazakhstan explained that the economic reform areas the firm examined included the creditworthiness of the government in its ability to make payments.[56] A third representative of a firm that conducted business in both countries stated that areas of reform in Kazakhstan that had influenced the business decision included the ability to freely exchange currency and the ability to repatriate foreign currency.[57] This representative additionally stated that economic conditions in Uzbekistan were difficult, and that nonconvertibility of the currency as well as other obstacles such as contract registration, import tariffs, and excise duties were factors.[58] The following section will compare each country's progress in the area of banking reform that these representatives considered important to their business decisions.

## Finance and Banking Sector Reform

The development of effective financial systems has been called a "central challenge" for the transition economies, mainly because banks under the Soviet system did not make decisions on credit based on the ability to repay (EBRD 1995, 19). Thus, the transformation of the banking sector is an indicator of progress toward a market economy. Kazakhstan, for example, adopted new banking legislation in August 1995 that confirmed the independence of the central bank and provided for the adoption of Bank for International Settlement (BIS) guidelines (EBRD 1996, 184). Uzbekistan's banking sector was still dominated by the state banks as of 2001, and intervention by the government in this sector included limits on cash withdrawals of both domestic and foreign currency deposits (EBRD 2001c, 211). Kazakhstan has overall made greater progress in liberalizing banking than Uzbekistan, as indicated in table 14.

The largest rating differential between the two countries first occurs in 1997, although Kazakhstan has been making steady progress, with rating increases in 1995, 1997, 2001, and 2003. Kazakhstan's rating improvement in 1997 can likely be explained by the decision of the government to agree to currency convertibility in 1996. In contrast, Uzbekistan's rating has not improved for any time period

**TABLE 14. EBRD RATING OF BANKING REFORM AND INTEREST RATE LIBERALIZATION FOR KAZAKHSTAN AND UZBEKISTAN**

| YEAR | KAZAKHSTAN | UZBEKISTAN |
|------|------------|------------|
| 1991 | 1.00 | 1.00 |
| 1992 | 1.00 | 1.00 |
| 1993 | 1.00 | 1.00 |
| 1994 | 1.00 | 1.00 |
| 1995 | 2.00 | 1.67 |
| 1996 | 2.00 | 1.67 |
| 1997 | 2.33 | 1.67 |
| 1998 | 2.33 | 1.67 |
| 1999 | 2.33 | 1.67 |
| 2000 | 2.33 | 1.67 |
| 2001 | 2.67 | 1.67 |
| 2002 | 2.67 | 1.67 |
| 2003–08 | 3.00 | 1.67 |

CLASSIFICATION SYSTEM FOR TRANSITION INDICATORS: BANKING REFORM AND INTEREST RATE LIBERALIZATION

1. Little progress beyond establishment of a two-tier system.
2. Significant liberalization of interest rates and credit allocation; limited use of directed credit or interest rate liberalization ceilings.
3. Substantial progress in establishment of bank solvency and of a framework for prudential supervision and regulation; full interest rate liberalization with little preferential access to cheap refinancing; significant lending to private enterprises and significant presence of private banks.
4. Significant movement of banking laws and regulations towards BIS standards; well-functioning banking competition and effective prudential supervision; significant term lending to private enterprises; substantial financial deepening. (EBRD 1998, 27)

NOTE: The classification system for the transition indicator scores has been modified from previous reports. Previous '+' and '–' ratings are treated by adding 0.33 and subtracting 0.33 from the full value. Averages are obtained by rounding down, for example, a score of 2.6 is treated as 2+, but a score of 2.8 is treated as 3– (EBRD 2007). These changes were made by the author for ease of comparison.

SOURCE: EBRD 2008.

after 1995, up to and including the assertion by the Uzbek government in 2003 to agree to currency convertibility, which is an additional indicator of broader problems in the banking sector. In other words, full account convertibility has not been implemented.

Therefore, it is unlikely that the decision by the Uzbek government to agree to currency convertibility in October 2003 will have a positive impact on the business climate in the country, for two reasons. First, businesses were already able to mitigate their nonconvertibility risks as long as the financing could be arranged. Second, in consultations with Uzbekistan, the IMF executive board noted that "serious restrictions in foreign as well as domestic trade remain" even though currency convertibility had "stimulated" economic activity in 2004.[59] These continued restrictions on trade and currency convertibility were confirmed during May and June 2005 in my follow-up communications with representatives of business firms who had been previously interviewed.[60] They explained that the situation had not improved, saying,

> While a stable currency would be better for the future, there was not much of an improvement right now.
>
> Little has changed. Yes there is convertibility in theory, but it is still very difficult to convert. You need to register contracts, wait for money to be available, etc. It is still a terrible place to do business. We pay all taxes and duties, which makes things even more difficult.
>
> Uzbek currency is *not* easily convertible. You have to get National Bank approval for each transaction. A lot of limitations. We do not see any positive move regarding liberalization of the country economy.

This assessment of the situation in Uzbekistan was confirmed in a study conducted by economists at the IMF during the summer of 2005. Its authors note that while the decision on currency convertibility was a "major step toward liberalizing the foreign exchange market," problems remain:

> These problems are largely twofold. First, enterprises reportedly have some difficulties converting sums into foreign exchange, since the CBU [Central Bank of Uzbekistan] makes foreign exchange available for the purchase of consumer goods only during the first few days of the month. Any outstanding applications for conversion after this initial period are held until the next month. Second, the conversion for some goods faces longer delays than others. Some reports indicate that the authorities are prohibiting conversion to finance prepayment for some imports. The CBU denies that convertibility restrictions exist, despite confirmation from local and international businessmen, private bankers and diplomats. (Gemayel and Grigorian 2005, 6)

The authors additionally state that if these restrictions were confirmed, they would be a violation of Article VIII of the IMF's Articles of Agreement, to which Uzbekistan had agreed to in moving to currency convertibility. While the decision on currency convertibility of the current account was a necessary step for economic progress in Uzbekistan, it does not appear, thus far, to have been a sufficient one in creating a stable business environment in the country.[61] This is in part because convertibility has not been carried out completely and because convertibility also requires fundamental reform in the overall business

TABLE 15. FIRMS' PERCEPTIONS OF ECONOMIC REFORM AND RISK

| TYPE OF FIRM | LEVEL OF RISK; IMPORTANCE OF ECONOMIC REFORM | WAY IN WHICH RISK IS ALLEVIATED |
|---|---|---|
| Natural Resource | High | Foreign investment laws, contract legislation, PSAs |
| Service | Low | Rely on direct investing firms; contract stipulates immediate payment |
| Business | Moderate | Private sector financing; or through US Ex-Im Bank, which provides guarantees or insurance for 85% of a privately financed loan contract |

climate, including banking sector reform and the lifting of trade restrictions. These policies are necessary for a country to move from an economy in which the state is heavily involved in economic decisions, to a free-market economy.

### ASSESSING RISK

The most notable difference between the three types of firms is their response to the question (2): "Did the country's implementation of economic reform influence the investment decision?" The representatives from the natural resources firms were concerned about the economic and political risks posed by their decisions and mitigated this risk by considering reforms related to contractual and investment legislation. Representatives of services firms, on the other hand, were not concerned about economic reform because their involvement with the countries was primarily through the contracts that they had arranged with the natural resource firms. Finally, while the representatives of business firms were concerned about the overall business environment, including currency convertibility in Uzbekistan, they were able to mitigate associated risks by using the U.S. Export-Import Bank to secure financing. The bank was used in Kazakhstan primarily for larger business deals that could not be secured through private sector finance. Therefore, each type of firm assessed its level of risk and looked for avenues to alleviate it (see table 15).

Having said this, there is a big difference between the level of risk associated with investing billions of dollars in a country's infrastructure, and the level associated with simply doing business with a country. This explains why firms were willing to do business with Uzbekistan despite its currency nonconvertibility, unreformed banking sector, and poor business climate overall. The financing support provided by the Ex-Im Bank undoubtedly increased business and the export of products, business activity that would not have been possible through private sector financing. These economic activities increased domestic business and employment in Uzbekistan, resulting in spillover effects. Such spillovers are most often seen as a result of direct investment, but they occurred in both Uzbekistan and Kazakhstan through a financing arrangement that allowed manufacturing to be done in the host countries. It is unfortunate that Uzbekistan has not taken advantage of opportunities to embrace market-style reforms and to improve its overall business climate.

# Conclusion

The reform paths of Kazakhstan and Uzbekistan must be analyzed within the historical, political, and economic framework of their status as former Soviet republics. Their different legacies best explain their divergent processes of reform. This book differs from previous studies because it details how each country's legacy influenced its economic policies, combining these historical indicators with economic data on each country's progress on reform in order to analyze its transition process. Earlier studies (Åslund, Boone, and Johnson 1996; Fish 1998) that relied on categorization of the regime type (democratic or non-Communist) were not able to predict adequately the continuation of economic reform in Kazakhstan. Even though Nazarbayev was part of the Communist-era elite, he followed through on reform. Additionally, decisions made about economic policies in both countries depend in part on their level of integration with Soviet-era Russia. Jeromin Zettlemeyer's paper "The Uzbek Growth Puzzle" (1998) explains much about why Uzbekistan's output fell less than any other former Soviet republic even though it did not proceed with rapid economic reforms. However, Zettlemeyer does not point out that Uzbekistan was less integrated than was Kazakhstan with Soviet-era Russia in key economic sectors. Consequently, Uzbekistan's lack of structural dependence provided the Uzbek government with flexibility on reform policy because at independence the country could continue to function at the same economic level.

Admittedly, this structural component only provides part of the explanation for the decision-making processes of these two states because it leaves the leaders and the elite in the proverbial "black box." Therefore, I have incorporated both of these key components of the decision-making process: the elite and the Soviet structural system. One way to do so is to use a variant of the agent-structure concept.[1] The agent-structure theory accounts for the "powers of agents" and the "structural factors" or conditions that necessarily shape an action carried out by a decision maker (Dessler 1989; Wendt 1987). In other words, the conditions under which decision makers operate are also necessary to explain the actions of those agents or decision makers. When Marx said, "People make history but not in conditions of their own choosing," he could not have known how true this would be for the future of the fifteen republics that comprised the Soviet structure. In fact, it was the longer legacies of democratic governments and market economies that partly explain why the CEE and Baltic states proceeded much more quickly with reform than the former Soviet states. As Amanda Wooden and Christoph Stefes (2009, 249) comment: "Post-Soviet societies did not start from scratch. Instead, their transitions from communism were embedded in numerous social, economic and political legacies. The legacies of the Soviet and pre-Soviet past have continued to shape developments of the post-Soviet present."

Indeed, the first survey of business leaders conducted by the EBRD and the World Bank in 1999 measured the extent to which the legacy of central planning was still dominant in the post-Communist countries. As discussed in the previous chapter, some of the responses from the business community were surprising. Notably, the slowest reformers and the most advanced reformers both ranked high on issues of governance, leaving the partial reformers ranked lower. While the survey's authors explained that this result by means of the similar capabilities of both the advanced and the slowest reformers to provide services that private firms need, they suggest that a different type of analysis is required: "While this interpretation is consistent with the facts, it does not provide an explanation as to why states differ in their willingness and capacity to undertake the institutional and behavioural reforms necessary to enhance market-oriented governance" (EBRD 1999, 117).

Some two decades after the end of the command economic system followed by the countries of the Soviet Union, we have a general understanding of the types of policies that these states have pursued. At this point, perhaps at least some the gradualists and the shock therapists are ready to concede that what is required is a mix of both policies. Mitchell Orenstein's (2001) finding that Poland and the Czech Republic successfully followed a blend of policies, what he calls "democratic policy alternation," certainly adds support to that proposal.

Now, however, it is more important to understand why some of the transition states continued with reform policies and why some did not. The following sections summarize the main findings of this book and provide explanations of that phenomenon.

## Summary of Findings

First, the Kazakh government under Nazarbayev had stronger motivations to implement reform policies than did the Uzbek government under Karimov. These motivations can be broadly defined under three components: structural, political, and economic. Chapter 1 outlined the structural components of reform and showed that differences between each republic's level of integration with Soviet-era Russia was a factor in determining its efforts at reform. Kazakhstan was more integrated with Soviet-era Russia in areas such as its electrical power grid, coal systems, and more importantly, oil and gas pipeline structures. The government of Kazakhstan, led by Nazarbayev, had to decide whether to continue operating with Russia's system or to engage the international community through market reforms. Uzbekistan, on the other hand, was the third largest producer of natural gas in the former Soviet Union; importantly, the production of gas was primarily for domestic industry, and very little was exported to Russia. Uzbekistan's gold and raw cotton, which the government exported, also provided important sources of revenue for the state. Therefore, the government of Uzbekistan, led by Karimov, did not depend on an integrated system with Russia in order to function at the same economic level after independence. In this context, the government decided to halt progress in market reforms.

The political components of reform involve the relationship that each leader had with his respective former first party secretary, which helped determine whether he looked to the past or to the future as a basis for reform. This component of reform was shaped more by the Soviet-era structure in Uzbekistan than it was in Kazakhstan. The relationship between Uzbekistan and Soviet-era Russia was strained as a result of Rashidov's falsifying the level of cotton production and the resulting Cotton Affair. While Moscow portrayed the Cotton Affair as a matter of corruption and bribery, the Uzbeks in Tashkent viewed the prosecution of Uzbeks as unfair. In reality, Rashidov and other leaders were forced to falsify the amounts of cotton delivered to Moscow if they wanted to keep their position. Inflating the quantity of goods delivered to Moscow was common practice in many of the Soviet republics—the Uzbeks just got caught. Policies that focused on cotton growing and production continued under Karimov, with support predominately from the Soviet-era elite.

Chapter 2 explained that while the Uzbek leadership moved forward initially with efforts at reform, these policies were reversed when there were severe balance-of-payments problems, and a decision was made to restrict access to foreign exchange. Other distorted policies were also kept in place, including Soviet-style state order systems for cotton and grain, and state control over the banking system. The reversal in reform policies, indeed the overall trajectory of reform in Uzbekistan, is best explained by Joel Hellman's (1998) theory of the politics of partial reform: the economy "stalls" in a partial reform state so that rents can be generated for the elite.

In Kazakhstan, Nazarbayev largely disassociated himself from Kunayev and his policies, which meant that he was also disassociating himself from the former Soviet elite. One of the most important and compelling differences between the political trajectories in Kazakhstan and Uzbekistan is the behavior of the country's parliament: Kazakhstan's legislature asserted itself under Nazarbayev, whereas Uzbekistan's was compliant under Karimov. In Kazakhstan the conflict emerged because Nazarbayev did not have the agreement of the consolidated elite in agreement on his reform policies.

Chapter 3 showed that Nazarbayev's decision to dissolve parliament and to rule by presidential decree was intended to get significant economic reforms implemented. Make no mistake: Nazarbayev's manipulations of the political system were all to his own benefit, including the "disbanding" of the parliament in 1993, the "decision" by the Constitutional Court that the parliamentary elections held in 1994 were invalid, and the decision to rule by presidential decree from March to December 1995. Certainly these actions were not openly democratic, but at various times Nazarbayev sought out some degree of institutional support or justification for his actions. For example, he did convince the 1993 parliament to disband (because of differences over reform policies); the court did decide that the elections were invalid; and during his rule by presidential decree, the new constitution was submitted for a vote by referendum (and passed). At best this could be considered managed democracy, but it is still in stark contrast to the operation of the political system in Uzbekistan. The fact that Kazakhstan will hold the chairmanship of the OSCE in 2010 also says something about the differences in the political systems of the two countries.

The economic components of reform must be considered within the political environment in which they occur. In all of the transition countries, moving from a command to a market-based economy involved calculations of the benefits that would flow to different groups as a result of the transition. The elite in Uzbekistan believed that it was best served by accruing rents from distorted economic policies, while the new elite in Kazakhstan believed that benefits would be derived from reform. Most notably, Nazarbayev and the new elite understood that reform policies would be needed to attract foreign investment and business. Even though some Kazakh legislation was geared toward specific sectors of the economy, important legal and regulatory frameworks were required for foreign investment, including privatization legislation, banking reform, and mechanisms for dispute settlement. There was a much greater overall commitment to reform in Kazakhstan than in Uzbekistan. The analysis presented in chapter 4 illustrated these differences. Responses from the representatives of firms whom I interviewed also confirm a greater overall commitment to reform in Kazakhstan than in Uzbekistan.

## Broader Policy Implications

The findings of this book have important implications for understanding the processes of economic reform in other transitioning or closed economies, as well as the relationships among reform, investment, and business. Paths of reform cannot be predicted solely by the political background of a leader (that is, whether he or she is former Communist or authoritarian). Instead, it is important to analyze a leader's history, along with writings and speeches that specifically address economic reform. Whom the leader chooses to serve in government is an additional predictor of whether the leader will continue with past policies or look to the future for reform.

Milan Svolik's (2008; 2009, 478) work on power sharing in authoritarian regimes illustrates the importance of political struggles among ruling authoritarian elites as a basis for analyzing policy decisions. Svolik focuses on why some authoritarian leaders are able to stay in power for decades, while others last for short periods of time. He argues that there is often a power struggle between the dictator and the ruling coalition that can result in various outcomes, two of which are generally applicable in Kazakhstan and Uzbekistan. In Kazakhstan, Nazarbayev worked to "increase his share of power relative to the power of the ruling coalition" and then "eliminate[ed] members of the ruling coalition" when he had sufficiently consolidated his power (Svolik 2009, 483). In Uzbekistan, on the other hand, Karimov worked more closely with the elite and consolidated his power with them, leading to a "transition from a contested to an established dictatorship" (Svolik 2009, 492).

The economic policies that a government pursues after an economic downturn are yet another strong indicator of the likelihood that a particular administration will continue to implement reforms or reverse direction. The financial crisis of 2008 will test both Karimov and Nazarbayev, but the latter has already made painful decisions on reform early in Kazakhstan's transition. Indeed, Bruce Pearlman and Gregory Gleason (2007) compare the administrative reform processes of Kazakhstan and Uzbekistan and conclude that their governments implemented very different reform policies. They attribute these differences to "policy choice rather than (shared) cultural values" and support Nazarbayev's policies, although Pearlman and Gleason do not investigate the factors responsible for the divergence in the two leaders' decisions (2007, 1339). Generally, research on Kazakhstan focuses less on its economic policy than on the potential for future problems flowing from its overreliance on the natural resource sector (Bayulgen 2009; Rumer 2005, 14–15; Pomfret 2005). While a diversified economy should be a concern for Kazakh citizens, especially with regards to equitable distribution of income, I strongly believe that their future is much brighter than that of Uzbeks, primarily because important economic reforms have been implemented in Kazakhstan.

Conversely, Uzbekistan's distorted economic policies cannot be sustained in the near future. Ultimately, changes in economic policies may have to be implemented by a new elite with different interests. Kobil Ruziev, Dipak Ghosh, and Sheila Dow (2007, 8) concur:

> Under the current regime it will not be possible to realise the true potential of the economy. The introduction of further reforms that can facilitate transition to a market economy and transform banking and financial institutions, will be the key, at this stage, to achieving sustainable economic growth in the future.

Much contemporary research on Uzbekistan still focuses on the validity of its early choices of economic policy. Most scholars believe that its partial reform policies (not gradualist) have been disastrous for Uzbek citizens. Deniz Kandiyoti, for example, remarks,

> Despite starting out with comparatively favourable indicators and more welfare oriented policies than its neighbours at the initial stages of transition, the partial reforms the government of Uzbekistan implemented in pursuit of stability

paradoxically created conditions of economic stagnation that required increased recourse to coercion. (2007, 44)

However, Martin Spechler (2007; 2008) asserts that Karimov's gradualist policies have been beneficial for the country and have helped prevent the economic crises that afflicted Russia. Again, this seems to be an argument about shock therapy versus gradualism, with Spechler taking the gradualist side. Kandiyoti's assessment of the need for "increased coercion" on the part of the Uzbek government seems borne out by the crackdown on Uzbek citizens in Andijon during May 2005. I believe that Uzbek citizens have a bleak future unless and until substantial reforms are implemented.

This book provides additional support for a correlation between the implementation of reform and increases in the level of investment and business. It presents evidence that specific reforms are likely to lead to investment, especially in the natural resource sector. In the case of Kazakhstan and Uzbekistan, investors also considered the potential size of the natural resource sector in each country. Abundant natural resources may encourage firms to negotiate a contract for exploration with the host government, but only if they have assurances through legislation that their investment will be secure. Serious attempts should be made to determine if governments understand what types of economic reform are desirable from the standpoint of investors. The degree to which stronger economic reforms can be shown to positively influence firms' willingness to do business in a country may affect how quickly those policies are implemented.

The most surprising finding from the interviews with business representatives was that Uzbekistan's lack of progress on reform did not result in fewer firms doing business in the country than in Kazakhstan.[2] While business firms do not invest the same level of assets as natural resource firms, I believed that Uzbekistan's lack of progress on tax legislation and banking sector reform constricted the number of firms doing business there. However, this was not the case because firms were able to secure financing through the U.S. Export-Import Bank, and in doing so, alleviate most of the commercial risk of doing business with the country. The financing support provided by export credit agencies such as the bank is an excellent way to increase business and employment opportunities in other transitioning and higher risk states.

It will be interesting to see how Kazakhstan and Uzbekistan change over the next twenty years. An important decision for their leaders is how to deal with the changing economic circumstances that have followed the 2008 financial crisis. Their leaders will also have to contend with changing geopolitical allegiances in the region and determine how strongly to align their country with Russia, the United States, or China. Finally, Nursultan Nazarbayev and Islam Karimov are currently the longest serving rulers from the Soviet era. An important test of the economic and political stability of their states will be the processes that bring in a new president, and the reform policies that the new leadership chooses.

# Notes

## INTRODUCTION

1. This statement was made during the author's interview with an IMF economist, July 8, 2002.
2. For examples of these studies see Citrin and Lahiri 1995; Wolf 1999; De Melo et al. 2001.
3. For an analysis of the IMF's influence in the reform policies implemented by Poland, Russia, Ukraine and Bulgaria see Stone 2002.
4. Åslund (2007, 54–55) also presents a scathing criticism of Joseph Stiglitz's reasons for supporting gradualism in Russia.
5. Following Cummings's (2005, 10–12) framework to identify the Kazakh elite.
6. World Bank economist, interview by the author, July 12, 2002
7. Murphy (2006, 552–54) termed this group the "Nazarbayev-led elite."
8. IMF Approves Three-Year Extended Fund Facility for Kazakhstan, IMF Press Release No. 96/39, July 17, 1996.
9. See the studies by Cummings (2005) and Murphy (2006).
10. IMF economist, interview by the author, July 9, 2002.
11. Kyrgyzstan's early progress on economic reform was primarily attributed to the fact that the country's president, Askar Akayev, was the only leader of the Central Asian states who had not been a first secretary of the Communist Party. However, this positive assessment of Akayev changed after irregularities in the 2000 parliamentary and presidential elections and the increasingly authoritarian policies he implemented. As a result of mass demonstrations owing to voting irregularities in the March 2005 parliamentary elections, Akayev fled the country and formally resigned as president

in April 2005 (see Isachenkov 2005).

## CHAPTER 1. BREAKING APART FROM RUSSIA

1. IMF 2003a, 5; Heather Timmons, "Oil Majors Agree to Develop a Big Kazakh Field," *New York Times*, February 26, 2004, W1, W7.

2. İpek (2007, 1183, 1188) also finds that Kazakhstan wanted to achieve economic independence from Russia in order to develop its own pipeline structure for exporting oil.

3. BP Statistical Review of World Energy, June 2008, p. 9.

4. Farangis Najibullah, "Moscow Seeking Alliances in Energy-Rich Central Asia," Radio Free Europe / Radio Liberty, September 4, 2008, at http://www.rferl.org/articleprintview/1196365.html.

5. Ibid. Also see the discussion in Pomfret 2006, 155–56, and the article by Sergei Blagov, "Investment Strengthens Russian Ties to Uzbekistan," at www.eurasia.net.org on August 4, 2004.

6. Farangis Najibullah, "Moscow Seeking Alliances in Energy-Rich Central Asia," Radio Free Europe / Radio Liberty, September 4, 2008, at http://www.rferl.org/articleprintview/1196365.html.

7. For an excellent analysis of the desiccation of the Aral Sea and the environmental and social consequences, see Small and Bunce 2003.

8. World Bank economist, interview by the author, July 10, 2002.

9. Only data for the years 1959, 1970, and 1971 were given for the demographic shifts in the population for the oblasts of Uzbekistan (Uzbek SSR Tsentral'noe statisticheskoe upravlenie 1971, 6).

10. Jonathan Birchall, "Wal-Mart Boycotts Uzbek Cotton," *Financial Times*, September 30, 2008.

11. Official from the Embassy of Uzbekistan, Washington, D.C., interview by the author, October 9, 2003.

12. Background information on cotton was provided by an expert on the cotton industry (interview by the author, September 25, 2003).

13. *Izvestia*, December 2, 1979, p. 5, *Current Digest of the Soviet Press* 30(49): 15–16; Ashkhabad Domestic Service in Russian, 13:15 GMT, November 17, 1982, Foreign Broadcast Information Service, November 17, 1982, p. T2.

14. *Pravda* (Moscow), in Russian, January 23, 1988, Second Edition, p. 3, Foreign Broadcast Information Service, January 28, 1988, p. 58.

15. See, for example, *Trud* (Moscow), in Russian, June 18 1988, p. 2, Foreign Broadcast Information Service, June 29, 1988, pp. 44–46; and *Tass* (Moscow), in English, 12:12 GMT, September 13, 1988, Foreign Broadcast Information Service, September 14,

1988, pp. 57–58.

16. In a meeting of the Uzbek Supreme Soviet on February 22, 1991, 241 cases of persons involved in the Cotton Affair were cleared; over 1,600 people involved in the Cotton Affair had already been rehabilitated (*Komsomolskaya Pravda* (Moscow), in Russian, April 2, 1991, p. 1, Foreign Broadcast Information Service, April 5, 1991, p. 75.

17. AFP (Paris), in English, 13:28 GMT, December 15, 1985, Foreign Broadcast Information Service, January 10, 1986, p. R6.

18. *Le Monde* (Paris), in French, December 21–22, 1986, p. 4, Foreign Broadcast Information Service, December 23, 1986, p. R2.

19. Critchlow 1991a, 27–28. This is not to say that Kunayev did not appoint loyal Kazakhs to important positions, including family members and members of his clan, but this was common practice in all the republics, and Kunayev's advancement of Kazakhs was not on the same scale as with similar sorts of appointments in Uzbekistan.

20. *Moscow News*, in English, no. 14, April 3, 1988, p. 13, Foreign Broadcast Information Service, April 13, 1988, pp. 50–52. Rashidov died in 1986 under circumstances that remain unexplained.

21. Interfax (Moscow), in English, 14:20 GMT, December 10, 1991, Foreign Broadcast Information Service, December 11, 1991, p. 81.

22. *Central Television First Program Network* (Moscow), in Russian, 20:55 GMT, October 24, 1991, Foreign Broadcast Information Service, October 29, 1991, pp. 74–75.

## CHAPTER 2. AGREEING TO MANAGE ECONOMIC POLICIES IN UZBEKISTAN

1. Moscow, Domestic Service, in Russian, 11:00 GMT, June 23, 1989, Foreign Broadcast Information Service, June 26, 1989, p. 70.

2. Tashkent, Domestic Service, in Uzbek, 01:15 GMT, March 30, 1986, Foreign Broadcast Information Service, March 31, 1986, pp. R10–R11; TASS International Service (Moscow), in Russian, 16:12 GMT, March 26, 1990, Foreign Broadcast Information Service, March 27, 1990, p. 121.

3. TASS International Service (Moscow), in Russian, 14:35 GMT, March 24, 1990, Foreign Broadcast Information Service, March 26, 1990, p. 137.

4. Donald Carlisle (1995, 198) explains that a reliable Uzbek source told him that the struggle was "between two bears that could not continue unresolved much longer."

5. Interfax (Moscow), in English, 10:55 GMT, August 15, 1991, Foreign Broadcast Information Service, August 16, 1991, p. 60; also see Carlisle 1995, 198.

6. TASS International Service (Moscow), in Russian, 14:35 GMT, March 24, 1990, Foreign Broadcast Information Service, March 26, 1990, p. 137.

7. *Izvestiya* (Moscow), in Russian, December 11, 1990, Foreign Broadcast Information

Service, December 14, 1990, p. 102.

8. Official with the Embassy of Uzbekistan, Washington, D.C., interview by the author, July 11, 2002.

9. *Izvestiya* (Moscow), in Russian, September 18, 1991, Foreign Broadcast Information Service, September 25, 1991, p. 90.

10. Official with the Embassy of Uzbekistan, Washington, D.C., interview by the author, July 11, 2002.

11. Http://www.gov.uz/eng/constitution/index.shtml.

12. Tashkent Domestic Service, in Uzbek, 02:15 GMT, October 28, 1987, Foreign Broadcast Information Service, November 9, 1987, p. 60.

13. Tashkent, *Pravda Vostoka,* in Russian, February 21, 1986, Foreign Broadcast Information Service, March 31, 1986, p. R13.

14. During the Soviet era, an appointment in the Uzbek construction sector was an important and sometimes lucrative position. During the early purges of the Uzbek elite, the head of the Ministry of Construction was accused of abusing his position for his "personal enrichment" (*Pravda Vostoka,* November 22, 1986, pp. 2–3, in *Current Digest of the Soviet Press* 37[51]: 5). Nancy Lubin has pointed out that corruption was common in the construction sector in Uzbekistan because it was easy to steal materials and resell them (1984, 193). Iskandarov and Mahamadalyev were both removed from the government in December 1998. I could not find information on why they were both removed at this time, but there was no person listed as minister of construction in December 1998, and in fact, the ministry did not exist after this time. In December 1999, a new Ministry of Housing and Municipal Economy was established with a new minister (REFFA 2000, 451).

15. *Nezavisimaya Gazeta* (Moscow), in Russian, June 28, 1994, p. 3, Foreign Broadcast Information Service, June 29, 1994, p. 55.

16. *Narodnoye Slovo* (Tashkent), in Russian, November 9, 1994, p. 1, Foreign Broadcast Information Service, November 9, 1994, p. 54.

17. IMF Approves Stand-by Credit and Second STF Drawing for the Republic of Uzbekistan, IMF Press Release, No. 95/67, December 18, 1995 (emphasis added). The STF, Structural Transformation Facility, was available only to transition economies, with no conditionality attached. The STF lapsed in 1995.

18. Uzbekistan held its first legislative elections in December 1994, for 250 seats in the Oliy Majlis. However, these elections were not considered free or fair, and the candidates largely supported the president (Freedom House 1998, 645). There is a general pattern in the implementation of laws in Uzbekistan. First a presidential decree is issued on a topic. Shortly thereafter, the Cabinet of Ministers passes a decree on the same topic, usually within a few months and with only a slight variation in

the title from the presidential decree.

19. IMF 2000a, 41. A study by the World Bank also confirmed that land had been reallocated for wheat at the expense of cotton, resulting in decreases in cotton production and increases in wheat production (Guadagni et al. 2005, 9).

20. IMF Approves Stand-by Credit and Second STF Drawing for the Republic of Uzbekistan, IMF Press Release, No. 95/67, December 18, 1995.

21. IMF economist, interview by the author, July 8, 2002.

22. IMF economists, interview by the author, July 9, 2002; World Bank economist, interview by the author, July 10, 2002.

23. IMF economist, interview by the author, July 8, 2002; official from the Embassy of Uzbekistan, Washington, D.C., interview by the author, July 11, 2002.

24. Http://uzland.narod.ru/gov_staf.htm for 2005 data; and http:www.uzland.uz/gov_staf.htm for data before 2000 and through 2004.

25. IMF economist, interview by the author, July 8, 2002; official from the Embassy of Uzbekistan, Washington, D.C., interview by the author, July 11, 2002.

26. On March 2, 2009, Raul Castro, as the president of Cuba fired some of his brother's (Fidel) closest aides, many with close ties to Fidel. However, analysts speculated that bringing new people into office does not necessarily mean a change politically or socially. Fidel subsequently made a speech indicating that those ousted had been too focused on their personal ambitions (Marc Lacey, "Amid a Lackluster Review of His First Year, Cuba's Leader Jolts the Government," *New York Times*, March 4, 2009, A6).

27. IMF 2000a, 85; IMF economists, interview by the author, October 22, 2003.

28. IMF economists, interview by the author, October 22, 2003.

29. IMF economists, interview by the author, October 22, 2003.

30. IMF Articles of Agreement, Article VIII.

31. IMF economists, interview by the author, October 22, 2003.

32. EBRD updates strategy for Uzbekistan, April 6, 2004, http://www.ebrd.com/new/pressrel/2004/44apri16.htm.

33. EBRD updates strategy for Uzbekistan, April 6, 2004, http://www.ebrd.com/new/pressrel/2004/44apri16.htm.

34. Daniel Kimmage, "Uzbek Police Crush Protest in Tashkent," Radio Free Europe/Radio Liberty, May 10, 2005; Bagila Bukharbayeva, "Hundreds Dead in Uzbek Uprising," *Moscow Times*, May 16, 2005, 1.

35. *New York Times*, April 1, 2010, B11.

36. Uzbekistan Country Brief October 2008, World Bank, http://go.worldbank.org/3L4POK4NQO.

37. Welfare Improvement Strategy of Uzbekistan, Tashkent 2007, annex 3, p. xii.

38. For additional information and analysis see Rumer 2005, 28–31.

## CHAPTER 3. ECONOMICS DETERMINES POLITICS FOR NAZARBAYEV

1. Vronskaya and Chuguev 1992, 357; TASS International Service (Moscow), in Russian, 09:54 GMT, June 22, 1989, Foreign Broadcast Information Service, June 22, 1989, p. 56.

2. TASS International Service (Moscow), in Russian, 09:54 GMT, June 22, 1989, Foreign Broadcast Information Service, June 22, 1989, p. 56.

3. Gorbachev's drive to end what he viewed as corrupt elite networks likely influenced the decision to promote a Russian and not a Kazakh. Also see Olcott 1995.

4. *Pravda* (Moscow), in Russian, March 5, 1986, pp. 4–5, Foreign Broadcast Information Service, March 14, 1986, pp. 9–10.

5. *Pravda* (Moscow), in Russian, February 23, 1990, p. 2, Foreign Broadcast Information Service, April 5, 1990, p. 120.

6. *Komsomolskaya Pravda* (Moscow), in Russian, April 13, 1991, p. 2, Foreign Broadcast Information Service, April 18, 1991, p. 59.

7. Press Association (London), in English, 20:28 GMT, October 28, 1991, Foreign Broadcast Information Service, October 29, 1991, p. 72.

8. Official from the Embassy of Kazakhstan, Washington, D.C., interview by the author, July 11, 2002.

9. *Komsomolskaya Pravda* (Moscow), in Russian, April 13, 1991, p. 2, Foreign Broadcast Information Service, April 18, 1991, p. 54.

10. For additional information, see Olcott 2002, 90–91.

11. Baker 1995, 658–65. Baker (1995, 581) also states that Nazarbayev had requested Western expertise in order to help transform Kazakhstan's economy.

12. As reported by Alma-Ata Kazakh Radio Network in Kazakh and Russian, 10:09 GMT, n December 10, 1991, Foreign Broadcast Information Service, December 11, 1991, p. 82.

13. *Izvestiya* (Moscow), in Russian, November 22, 1990, Foreign Broadcast Information Service, November 23, 1990, p. 54.

14. Daulet Sembaev was also an economist. See Cummings 2005, 23–24.

15. *Sotsialistik Zazaqstan* (Alma-Ata), in Kazakh, June 6, 1990, p. 1, Foreign Broadcast Information Service, June 15, 1990, p. 132.

16. Interfax (Moscow), in English, 17:33 GMT, November 22, 1993, Foreign Broadcast Information Service, November 23, 1993, p. 62.

17. Yet he would also describe the parliament elected in 1994 as "unwieldy" and "unable to function" (*Kommersant-Daily*, July 6, 1995, p. 4, *Current Digest of the Post-Soviet Press*

47[27]: 21).

18. For detailed analysis of this situation as well as the similarities in the governing styles of Yeltsin and Nazarbayev see Furman 2005, especially 206–10.

19. Kazakh Radio Network (Almaty), in Russian, 08:00 GMT, May 30, 1994, Foreign Broadcast Information Service, May 31, 1994, p. 74.

20. Kazakh Radio Network (Almaty), in Russian, 08:00 GMT, May 30, 1994, Foreign Broadcast Information Service, May 31, 1994, p. 74.

21. Kazakh Radio Network (Almaty), in Kazakh, 08:00 GMT, May 31, 1994, Foreign Broadcast Information Service, May 31, 1994, p. 75.

22. Interfax (Moscow), in English, 11:02 GMT, May 31, 1994, Foreign Broadcast Information Service, June 1, 1994, p. 52.

23. IMF Approves Stand-by Credit for Kazakhstan, Press Release No. 94/2, January 1994.

24. Kazakh Radio Network (Almaty), in Kazakh, 14:00 GMT, May 31, 1994, Foreign Broadcast Information Service, June 1, 1994, p. 51.

25. Interfax (Moscow), in English, 16:35 GMT, June 2, 1994, Foreign Broadcast Information Service, June 3, 1994, p. 56.

26. *Kaztag* (Almaty), in Russian, 13:00 GMT, June 14, 1994, Foreign Broadcast Information Service, June 15, 1994, p. 49.

27. Kazakh Radio Network (Almaty), in Kazakh, 14:00 GMT, June 14, 1994, Foreign Broadcast Information Service, June 15, 1994, p. 49.

28. See Kazakh Radio Network (Almaty), in Russian, 14:00 GMT, June 17 1994, Foreign Broadcast Information Service, June 20, 1994, p. 61; Kazakh Radio Network (Almaty), in Kazakh, 14:00 GMT, June 17, 1994, Foreign Broadcast Information Service, June 20, 1994, p. 61.

29. Interfax (Moscow), in English, 15:30 GMT, June 22, 1994, Foreign Broadcast Information Service, June 23, 1994, p. 50.

30. Itar-Tass (Moscow), in English, 12:22 GMT, June 22, 1994, Foreign Broadcast Information Service, June 23, 1994, p. 50.

31. *Pravda*, September 23, 1994, p. 1, *Current Digest of the Post-Soviet Press* 46(38): 23.

32. Sevodnya Business News Agency, October 12, 1994, p. 1, *Current Digest of the Post-Soviet Press* 46(41): 23.

33. Sevodnya Business News Agency, October 13, 1994, p. 5, *Current Digest of the Post-Soviet Press* 46(41): 24.

34. Sevodnya Business News Agency, October 13, 1994, p. 5, *Current Digest of the Post-Soviet Press* 46(41): 23.

35. *Sovety Kazakhstana* (Almaty), in Russian, December 28, 1994, p. 1, Foreign Broadcast Information Service, January 5, 1995, p. 36.

36. Basically the court ruled that the constitution had been violated in one district, and

voided the entire election results. For more detailed information, see Furman 2005, 213–14 and Cummings 2005, 26.

37. *Nezavisimaya gazeta*, March 21, 1995, p. 1, *Current Digest of the Post-Soviet Press* 47(12): 24.

38. Kazakh Television First Program Network (Almaty), in Russian, 15:07 GMT, March 24, 1995, Foreign Broadcast Information Service, March 27, 1995, pp. 68–70.

39. Sevodnya, July 22, 1995, p. 4, *Current Digest of the Post-Soviet Press* 47(29): 20.

40. Japan's constitution has a similar risk for a vote of no confidence in the government. In Japan's parliamentary system, the lower house, the House of Representatives, has the power to pass a no-confidence vote in the cabinet; the government then has a choice to either dissolve the lower house within 10 days (leading to new elections for the lower house), or the cabinet resigns and the prime minister forms a new cabinet.

41. Http://www.kz/eng/kzinfo/CONST/CONSTENG/ukaz1.htm.

42. *Kommersant-Daily*, September 1, 1995, p. 3, *Current Digest of the Post-Soviet Press* 47(35): 24.

43. *Kommersant-Daily*, July 6, 1995, p. 4, *Current Digest of the Post-Soviet Press* 47(27): 21.

44. *Kommersant-Daily*, July 6, 1995, p. 4, *Current Digest of the Post-Soviet Press* 47(27): 21.

45. As required by the Articles of Agreement of the IMF, Article VIII, sections 2 and 3.

46. IMF Approves Three-Year Extended Fund Facility for Kazakhstan, Press Release No. 96/39, July 17, 1996.

47. IMF economist, personal conversation, September 5, 2001; IMF economists, interview by the author, July 8 and 9, 2002.

48. Current information on the 2008 Kazakh government found at http://en.government.kz/structure/government.

49. This was part of a longer conversation that I had with a World Bank economist on July 12, 2002.

50. *Nezavisimaya gazeta*, December 8, 1995, p. 3, *Current Digest of the Post-Soviet Press* 47(49): 23.

51. For more detailed information on these events see Furman 2005, 224–30; Olcott 2002, 119–22.

52. OSCE 2006, 3. In light of this irregularity in the election, it is surprising that Kazakhstan will occupy the position of chair of the OSCE in 2010. Kazakhstan will be the first of the former Soviet republics to do so and with the support of the United States, in return for assurances that Kazakhstan will "protect" the election monitoring body of the OSCE that Russia had wanted to modify (RFE/RL, "Kazakhstan to Assume OSCE Chairmanship in 2010," December 1, 2007). The "special relationship" between the United States and Kazakhstan seems to have continued well past the conversation between James Baker and Nazarbayev about such a relationship in 1992.

53. RFE/RL, "Kazakh Deputies Approve Unlimited Terms for Nazarbayev," May 18, 2007.

54. World Bank Country Brief, Kazakhstan 2008, at http://www.go.worldbank. org/4SD88J44EO.

55. Literature on the resource curse is abundant. For information on how it has affected Kazakhstan, see Olcott 2002; Pomfret 2005; Bayulgen 2009.

56. Eurasianet.org, "Kazakhstan: Astana Acts Aggressively to Contain Financial Crisis," November 21, 2008.

57. Eurasianet.org, "Kazakhstan: IMF Official Praises Kazakhstani Bank Bailout Plan," November 19, 2008.

58. Eurasianet.org, "Kazakhstan: Astana Acts Aggressively to Contain Financial Crisis," November 21, 2008.

59. Eurasianet.org, "Kazakhstan: Astana Acts Aggressively to Contain Financial Crisis," November 21, 2008.

60. Eurasianet.org, "Kazakhstan: IMF Official Praises Kazakhstani Bank Bailout Plan," November 19, 2008.

## CHAPTER 4. CONNECTING SPECIFIC REFORM POLICIES TO INVESTMENT AND BUSINESS

1. Stern's (1995) chapter was part of a larger project (Dyker 1995) compiled from papers by the Post-Soviet Business Forum, which has provided support for publications and meetings with academics and businesspersons.

2. The 2001 EBRD *Transition Report* was titled "Energy in Transition," and chapter 4 in particular ("Managing Energy Resource Wealth") details the reform and investment climate challenges of the energy-rich countries, including Azerbaijan, Kazakhstan, Russia, Turkmenistan, and Uzbekistan.

3. For examples, see Auty 2001; Gelb and Associates 1988.

4. The states included in the study were Russia, Kazakhstan, Uzbekistan, Azerbaijan, and Turkmenistan (Weinthal and Jones Luong 2001, 215–16).

5. This conclusion is based on their assertion that domestic actors in Russia were helping to "foster the development of an increasingly viable tax regime in Russia," while in Kazakhstan "the tax regime has become increasingly volatile and dependent upon these foreign investors" (Weinthal and Jones Luong 2001, 215). It should be noted that this article was published before the Russian government became more involved in collecting alleged back taxes from private firms such as Yukos.

6. See, for example, Ebel and Menon 2000; Karl 2000. This was also suggested during an interview with consultants from DRI-WEFA (formerly Plan Econ) on July 11, 2002.

7. Interviews with representatives from large U.S. firms that had invested or conducted business in Kazakhstan and Uzbekistan were conducted in Washington, D.C., from

September to October 2003, with some follow-up interviews conducted in 2005. Specific information on the firms is provided in the section "Characteristics of Firms" as well as in table 11. Additional interviews were carried out during this period, as well as during June 2001 and July 2002, with other members of the business, governmental, and policy communities to complement the information provided by firm representatives. These interviews were conducted with officials at the Embassy of Kazakhstan, the Embassy of Uzbekistan, the American-Uzbekistan Chamber of Commerce, the U.S.-Kazakhstan Business Association, the U.S. Export-Import Bank, the U.S. Department of Commerce, and other trade officials.

8. For the combined years 1993–98, the United States was the largest foreign investor in Kazakhstan, at 32.9 percent of FDI (Gosudarstvennyi komitet Respubliki Kazakhstan po statistike i analizu, 1999, 117). The United States was also the largest investor in the years 1999–2001 (IMF 2003a, 103). Uzbekistan does not provide detailed information on its foreign direct investment by industry in the *Staff Country Reports* published by the IMF. Information provided to me by an official at the Embassy of Uzbekistan indicated that the industrial sector received the largest share of foreign investment and credits at 69.3 percent. The second largest sector was transportation at 12.4 percent, and a catchall category of "others" was third at 11.7 percent (information provided by the Embassy of the Republic of Uzbekistan, 2001). Information on the share of U.S. investment in Uzbekistan is not easily available. However, the cumulative (amounts are cumulative year after year) direct investment of U.S. firms for 1999 (data were suppressed for 1994–98) was $167 million (www.bea.gov). In personal correspondence with an official in the International Investment Division in the Bureau of Economic Analysis he explained that "[t]he BEA cannot publish any data that would reveal financial information about an individual company. So if a small number of companies are responsible for most of the data in a particular data item, we cannot publish that number" (Thomas Anderson, Bureau of Economic Analysis, correspondence with the author, November 17, 2003). Data were suppressed (denoted by a 'D' for the following years: 1994, 1995, 1996, 1997, and 1998. The amount listed for 1999 was $167 million. Cumulative direct foreign investment in Uzbekistan for the years 1994–99 was $567 million (EBRD 2001b, 68). Direct foreign investment in Uzbekistan for 1994–99 averaged $94.5 million per year, and U.S. direct investment averaged about $27.8 million per year; therefore U.S. direct investment in Uzbekistan was about 29 percent of FDI between 1994 and 1999.

9. Firms were identified from the following data sources: EBRD 2001a; 2001b; OECD 1996; OECD 1998; U.S.-Kazakhstan Business Association 2000. Officials at the Embassy of Uzbekistan as well as at the American-Uzbekistan Chamber of Commerce provided additional information on firms with investment and business in Uzbekistan (official

from the Embassy of Uzbekistan, Washington, D.C., interviews by the author, July 11, 2002, October 9, 2003; official from the Uzbekistan-American Chamber of Commerce, interviews by the author, July 11, 2002, October 30, 2003).

10. For additional information about the use of interviews as a research method for data collection see Dexter 1970, 5–7; Johnson and Joslyn 1995, 265; Aberdach and Rockman 2002, 673.

11. For an example of a previous study that used anonymous interviews with representatives from oil and gas companies see Jones Luong and Weinthal 2004.

12. Question (2) was asked before question (9) in all of the interviews. The first question asked in these interviews was "What was the primary reason for the investment decision in Kazakhstan/Uzbekistan?" This was asked in order to clarify the sectors of investment. The most common responses from these interviewees were "where the oil is," "country has reserves of natural gas," "where the gold is."

13. Anonymous, interview by the author, October 30, 2003.

14. Anonymous, interview by the author, October 30, 2003.

15. Representative of a natural resource firm, interview by the author, October 2, 2003.

16. Representative of a natural resource firm, interview by the author, October 2, 2003.

17. Representative of a natural resource firm, interview by the author, September 30, 2003.

18. Representative of a natural resource firm, interview by the author, October 14, 2003.

19. In 1993 the World Bank rated Uzbekistan's oil potential "significant" as a result of the discovery of fields in the Namagan and Fergana regions, although at the time production levels were minor (World Bank 1993b, 4–5). An IMF economist remarked that Uzbekistan may have larger reserves than are currently proven (interview by the author, July 9, 2002).

20. Representative of a natural resource firm, interview by the author, October 14, 2003.

21. Representative of a natural resource firm, interview by the author, September 23, 2003.

22. Representative of a natural resources firm, interview by the author, September 30, 2003.

23. Representative of a natural resource firm, interview by the author, September 30, 2003.

24. Representative of a natural resources firm, interview by the author, September 30, 2003. Stern (2005, 67–68) notes that presidents and prime ministers are also heavily involved in frameworks of agreement for natural gas deals in the CIS.

25. Representatives of service firms, interviews by the author, September–October 2003.

26. Representative of a natural resource firm, interview by the author, October 14, 2003.

27. Representatives of natural resource firms, interviews by the author, September–October

2003.

28. Russia and Eurasia Documents Annual 1995, 286; the complete decree is on pp. 286–99.

29. Representative of a natural resource firm, interview by the author, September 23, 2003.

30. Michael Lelyveld, "Kazakhstan: Western Fuel Investors Face Further Setbacks," REF/RL, October 29, 2001.

31. RFE/RL, "Nazarbayev Promises Investors no Revisions to Contracts . . . but not Adverse to Voluntary Donations," *RFE/RL Central Asia Report* 1(22): December 20, 2001.

32. Anonymous, interview by the author, October 22, 2003.

33. Anonymous, interview by the author, September 15, 2003.

34. Heather Timmons, "Oil Majors Agree to Develop a Big Kazakh Field," *New York Times* February 26, 2004, W1, W7.

35. Representative of a natural resource firm, interview by the author, September 23, 2003. The decision of the Kazakh government to agree to export some of its oil via the new Baku-Tblisi-Ceyhan (BTC) Pipeline will also increase the country's export potential. President Nazarbayev's official visit to the United States on September 29, 2006 to discuss, among other issues, a commitment to increase its oil exports through this pipeline is an indicator of the country's growing geopolitical strategic importance to the United States as well as to other countries, including China. For background information, see Joanna Lillis, "Nazarbayev Visit to Washington: Looking for Recognition as a Regional Leader," Eurasianet.org, September 26, 2006.

36. Official from the Embassy of Uzbekistan, interviews by the author, July 11, 2002, October 9, 2003; official from the Department of Commerce, interview by the author, October 16, 2003.

37. "Two Views of the New Uzbek Laws on Investors' Rights," at http://www.bisnis.doc.gov/bisnis/country/9807uzin.htm, accessed October 9, 2003.

38. Law of the Republic of Uzbekistan, "On Foreign Investments," April 30, 1998.

39. "Two Views of the New Uzbek Laws on Investors' Rights," at http://www.bisnis.doc.gov/bisnis/country/9807uzin.htm, accessed October 9, 2003.

40. See Law of the Republic of Uzbekistan, May 26, 2000, No. 77-II, on the introduction of amendments and supplements to Law of the Republic of Uzbekistan, "On Foreign Economic Activity of the Republic of Uzbekistan," legislation provided by the Embassy of Uzbekistan.

41. Anonymous, interview by the author, July 11, 2002.

42. This finding illustrates one of the many benefits of conducting focused personal interviews in addition to open-ended questions, even though the analysis of this

data is time consuming.

43. See the mission statement of the bank at http://www.exim.gov/about/mission.html.

44. See the chapters in Hufbauer and Rodriguez 2001.

45. Information on the bank's financing and position regarding Kazakhstan and Uzbekistan was provided in an interview with an Export-Import Bank economist on October 3, 2003.

46. Export-Import Bank economist, interview by the author, October 3, 2003.

47. Transactions that are short term usually involve a maximum credit period of 180 days; in some cases it can be extended to 360 days. Medium term generally begins at two years, and long term is traditionally a period of more than five years (Stephens 1999, 95, 108).

48. Export-Import Bank economist, interview by the author, October 3, 2003.

49. Representative of a business firm, interview by the author, September 30, 2003.

50. Representative of a business firm, interview by the author, September 24, 2003.

51. Representative of a business firm, interview by the author, October 16, 2003.

52. Representative of a business firm, interview by the author, October 16, 2003.

53. Anonymous, interview by the author, July 11, 2002.

54. Representative of a business firm, interview by the author, September 12, 2003; representative of a business firm, personal communication, December 1, 2003.

55. Representative of a business firm, interview by the author, October 30, 2003.

56. Representative of a business firm, interview by the author, September 12, 2003.

57. Representative of a business firm, personal communication, December 1, 2003.

58. Representative of a business firm, personal communication, December 1, 2003.

59. IMF Executive Board Concludes 2005 Article IV Consultation with Republic of Uzbekistan, IMF Public Information Notice No. 05/73, June 10, 2005.

60. Representatives of business firms, personal communications, June 20, 2005, May 31, 2005, June 9, 2005.

61. Economists from the IMF stated that the decision to agree to currency convertibility was "necessary but not sufficient" to boost economic growth, in part because of trade restrictions introduced in 2002 (interview by the author, October 22, 2003).

## CONCLUSION

1. I would like to thank Christoph Stefes for this suggestion.

2. There was only one firm that did not conduct business with both Uzbekistan and Kazakhstan (representative of a business firm, interview by the author, September 12, 2003).

# References

Abdelal, Rawi. 2001. *National Purpose in the World Economy: Post-Soviet States in Comparative Perspective.* Ithaca, N.Y.: Cornell University Press.

Aberdach, Joel, and Bert Rockman. 2002. Conducting and Coding Elite Interviews. *Political Science and Politics* 35(4): 673–78.

Alexandrov, Mikhail. 1999. *Uneasy Alliance: Relations between Russia and Kazakhstan in the Post-Soviet Era.* Westport, Conn.: Greenwood Press.

Amsden, Alice, Jacek Kochanowicz, and Lance Taylor. 1994. *The Market Meets Its Match: Restructuring the Economies of Eastern Europe.* Cambridge: Harvard University Press.

Åslund, Anders. 1989. Soviet and Chinese Reforms—Why They Must Be Different. *World Today* 45(11): 188–91.

———. 1992. *Post Communist Economic Revolutions: How Big a Bang?* Washington, D.C.: Center for Strategic and International Studies.

———. 1995. *How Russia Became a Market Economy.* Washington, D.C.: Brookings Institution.

———. 2002. *Building Capitalism: The Transformation of the Former Soviet Bloc.* Cambridge: Cambridge University Press.

———. 2007. *How Capitalism Was Built: The Transformation of Central and Eastern Europe, Russia and Central Asia.* Cambridge: Cambridge University Press.

Åslund, Anders, Peter Boone, and Simon Johnson. 1996. How to Stabilize: Lessons from Post-Communist Countries. *Brookings Papers on Economic Activity* 1:217–313.

Auty, Richard, ed. 2001. *Resource Abundance and Economic Development.* Oxford: Oxford University Press.

Baker, James III. 1995. *The Politics of Diplomacy: Revolution, War and Peace, 1989–1992.* New

York: G. P. Putnam's Sons.

Balcerowicz, Leszek. 1995. *Socialism, Capitalism, Transformation.* Budapest: Central European University Press.

Bayulgen, Oksan. 2009. Caspian Energy Wealth: A Curse or a Blessing for the Region? In *The Politics of Transition in Central Asia and the Caucasus: Enduring Legacies and Emerging Challenges,* ed. Amanda Wooden and Christoph Stefes. New York: Routledge.

Berg, Andrew, Eduardo Borensztein, Ratna Sahay, and Jeromin Zettelmeyer. 1999. The Evolution of Output in Transition Economies: Explaining the Differences. IMF Working Paper WP/99/73. Washington, D.C.: IMF.

Bevan, Alan, and Saul Estrin. 2004. The Determinants of Foreign Direct Investment into Europe and Transition Economies. *Journal of Comparative Economics* 32(4): 775–87.

Bevan, Alan, Saul Estrin, and Klaus Meyer. 2003. Foreign Investment Location and Institutional Development in Transition Economies. *International Business Review* 13:43–64.

Blackmon, Pamela. 2005. Back to the USSR: Why the Past Does Matter in Explaining the Differences in the Economic Reform Processes of Kazakhstan and Uzbekistan. *Central Asian Survey* 24(4): 391–404.

———. 2007. Divergent Paths, Divergent Outcomes: Linking Differences in Economic Reform to Levels of US Direct Foreign Investment and Business in Kazakhstan and Uzbekistan. *Central Asian Survey* 26 (3): 355–72.

———. 2009. Following Through on Reforms: Comparing Market Liberalization in Kazakhstan and Uzbekistan. In *The Politics of Transition in Central Asia and the Caucasus: Enduring Legacies and Emerging Challenges,* ed. Amanda Wooden and Christoph Stefes. New York: Routledge.

Brock, Gregory. 1998. Foreign Direct Investment in Russia's Regions 1993–1995: Why So Little and Where Has It Gone? *Economics of Transition* 3(4): 349–60.

Brukoff, Patricia. 1995. The Unwilling State: Exploring Kazakhstan's Resistance to Economic Autonomy in the Post-Soviet Period. Dissertation. Rand Corporation.

Bunce, Valerie, and John M. Echols III. 1980. Soviet Politics in the Brezhnev Era: "Pluralism" or "Corporatism." In *Soviet Politics in the Brezhnev Era,* ed. Donald Kelley. New York: Praeger, 1–26.

Carlisle, Donald. 1991. Power and Politics in Soviet Uzbekistan: From Stalin to Gorbachev. In *Soviet Central Asia: The Failed Transformation,* ed. William Fierman. Boulder: Westview Press.

———. 1995. Islam Karimov and Uzbekistan: Back to the Future? In *Patterns in Post-Soviet Leadership,* ed. Timothy J. Colton and Robert C. Tucker. Boulder: Westview Press.

Central Intelligence Agency (CIA). 1995. Comparative Ethnic Groups in the Former Soviet Union, 1989 (figure). Washington, D.C.: CIA.

Citrin, Danile, and Ashok Lahiri, eds. 1995. Policy Experiences and Issues in the Baltics,

Russia and Other Countries of the Former Soviet Union. International Monetary Fund, Occasional Paper 133. Washington, D.C.: IMF.

Collins, Kathleen. 2002. Clans, Pacts and Politics in Central Asia. *Journal of Democracy* 13(3): 137–52.

———. 2004a. The Political Role of Clans in Central Asia. *Comparative Politics* 35(2): 171–90.

———. 2004b. The Logic of Clan Politics: Evidence from the Central Asian Trajectories. *World Politics* 56(2): 224–61.

Commission on Security and Cooperation in Europe (CSCE). 1994. *Report on the March 7, 1994 Parliamentary Election in Kazakhstan.* Washington, D.C.: CSCE.

Committee for World Atlas of Agriculture. 1969. *World Atlas of Agriculture.* Vol. 1. Novara: Istituto Geografico De Agostini.

Commodity Research Bureau. 2000, 2003, 2007, 2008. Commodity Yearbook. New York: John Wiley and Sons.

Cook, Linda. 2007. *Postcommunist Welfare States: Reform Politics in Russia and Eastern Europe.* Ithaca, N.Y.: Cornell University Press.

Critchlow, James. 1988. "Corruption," Nationalism and the Native Elites in Soviet Central Asia. *Journal of Communist Studies* 4(2): 142–61.

———. 1991a. *Nationalism in Uzbekistan.* Boulder: Westview Press.

———. 1991b. Prelude to "Independence": How the Uzbek Party Apparatus Broke Moscow's Grip on Elite Recruitment. In *Soviet Central Asia,* ed. William Fierman. Boulder: Westview Press.

Cummings, Sally. 2005. *Kazakhstan: Power and the Elite.* London: I. B. Tauris.

Dawisha, Karen, and Bruce Parrott, eds. 1997. *Conflict, Cleavage and Change in Central Asia and the Caucasus.* Cambridge: Cambridge University Press.

Dessler, David. 1989. What's at Stake in the Agent-Structure Debate? *International Organization* 43(3): 441–73.

De Melo, Martha, Cevdet Denzier, Alan Gelb, and Stoyan Tenev. 2001. Circumstance and Choice: The Role of Initial Conditions and Policies in Transition Economies. *World Bank Economic Review* 15(1): 1–31.

Dexter, Lewis Anthony 1970. *Elite and Specialized Interviewing.* Evanston, IL: Northwestern University Press.

Dittmann, Katherian, Hella Engerer, and Christian von Hirschhausen. 2001. Much Ado about . . . Little? Disenchantment in the Kazak and Caspian Oil and Gas Sectors. In *Kazakhstan 1993–2000: Independent Advisors and the IMF,* ed. Lutz Hoffman, Peter Bofinger, Heiner Flassbeck, and Alfred Steinherr. New York: Physica-Verlag.

Dyker, David, ed. 1995. *Investment Opportunities in Russia and the CIS.* Washington, D.C.: Brookings Institution.

Easter, Gerald. 1997. Preference for Presidentialism: Postcommunist Regime Change in

Russia and the NIS. *World Politics* 49(2): 184–211.

Ebel, Robert, and Rajan Menon, eds. 2000. *Energy Conflict in Central Asia and the Caucasus.* Boulder: Rowman and Littlefield.

European Bank for Reconstruction and Development (EBRD). 1995–2009. *Transition Report.* London: EBRD.

———. 2001a. *Investment Profile Kazakhstan.* London: EBRD.

———. 2001b. *Investment Profile Uzbekistan.* London: EBRD.

———. 2001c. *Transition Report. London:* EBRD.

Falcetti, Elisabetta, Martin Raiser, and Peter Sanfey. 2000. Defying the Odds: Initial Conditions, Reforms and Growth in the First Decade of Transition. EBRD Working Paper No. 55. London: EBRD.

Fierman, William. 1997. Political Development in Uzbekistan: Democratization? In *Conflict, Cleavage and Change in Central Asia and the Caucasus,* ed. Karen Dawisha and Bruce Parrot. Cambridge: Cambridge University Press.

Fischer, Stanley. 1997. Applied Economics in Action: IMF Programs. *American Economic Review* 87(2): 23–27.

Fischer, Stanley, and Jacob Frenkel. 1992. Macroeconomic Issues of Soviet Reform. *American Economic Review* 82(2): 37–42.

Fischer, Stanley, and Alan Gelb. 1991. The Process of Socialist Economic Transformation. *Journal of Economic Perspectives* 5(4): 91–105.

Fischer, Stanley, and Ratna Sahay. 2000. The Transition Economies after Ten Years. IMF Working Paper WP/00/30. Washington, D.C.: IMF.

Fischer, Stanley, Ratna Sahay, and Carlos Vegh. 1996. Economies in Transition: The Beginnings of Growth. *American Economic Review* 86(2): 229–33.

Fish, Steven. 1998. The Determinants of Economic Growth in the Post-Communist World. *Eastern European Politics and Societies* 12(1): 31–78.

Forsythe, Rosemarie. 1996. The Politics of Oil in the Caucasus and Central Asia. Adelphi Paper 300, 1–67.

Freedom House. 1998. *Nations in Transit.* Ed. Adrian Karatnychy. New York: Freedom House.

———. 1999–2000. *Freedom in the World.* New York: Freedom House.

Furman, Dmitrii. 2005. The Regime in Kazakhstan. In *Central Asia at the End of the Transition,* ed. Boris Rumer. New York: M. E. Sharpe.

Gelb, Alan, and Associates. 1988. *Oil Windfalls: Blessing or Curse?* Oxford: Oxford University Press.

Gemayel, Edward R., and David A. Grigorian. 2005. How Tight Is Too Tight? A Look at Welfare Implications of Distortionary Policies in Uzbekistan. IMF Working Paper 05/239. Washington, D.C.: IMF.

Gilbert, Martin. 2002. *The Routledge Atlas of Russian History.* 3rd ed. London: Routledge.

Gleason, Gregory. 1997. *The Central Asian States.* Boulder: Westview Press.

———. 2001. Foreign Policy and Domestic Reform in Central Asia. *Central Asian Survey* 20(2): 167–82.

———. 2003a. *Markets and Politics in Central Asia: Structural Reform and Political Change.* New York: Routledge.

———. 2003b. Russia and the Politics of the Central Asian Electricity Grid. *Problems of Post-Communism* 50(3): 42–52.

Gomułka, Stanislaw. 1989. Shock Needed for Polish Economy. *The Guardian,* August 19.

Gosudarstvennyi komitet Respubliki Kazakhstan po statistike i analizu. 1999. *Kratkii statischeskii ezhegodnik Kazakhstana.* Almaty: Government of Kazakhstan.

Graham, Norman A. 2006. Introduction and overview. In *The Political Economy of Transition in Eurasia: Democratization and Economic Liberalization in a Global Economy,* ed. Norman A. Graham and Folke Lindahl. East Lansing: Michigan State University Press.

Guadagni, Maurizio, Martin Raiser, Anna Crole-Rees, and Dilshod Khidirov. 2005. Cotton Taxation in Uzbekistan: Opportunities for Reform. ECSSD Working Paper No. 41. Washington, D.C.: World Bank.

Gürgen, Emine. 2000. Central Asia: Achievements and Prospects. *Finance and Development* 37:40–43.

Hellman, Joel. 1998. Winners Take All: The Politics of Partial Reform in Postcommunist Transitions. *World Politics* 50(2): 202–34.

Hufbaer, Gary C., and Rita M. Rodriguez, eds. 2001. *The EX-IM Bank in the 21st Century: A New Approach?* Washington, D.C.: Institute for International Economics.

Husain, Aasim H. 2007. Sustaining Kazakhstan's Macroeconomic Success. *Kazakhstan's Echo* 34 (February 5): 1–3; reprinted from *Business and Power* (Kazakhstan), December 29, 2006.

International Monetary Fund (IMF). 1992. *Economic Review: Uzbekistan.* Washington, D.C.: IMF.

———. 1995. *Republic of Uzbekistan: Background Paper and Statistical Appendix.* Staff Country Report No. 95/23. Washington, D.C.: IMF.

———. 1996. *Republic of Kazakhstan: Recent Economic Developments.* Staff Country Report No. 96/22. Washington, D.C.: IMF.

———. 1997a. *Republic of Kazakhstan: Recent Economic Developments.* Staff Country Report No. 97/67. Washington, D.C.: IMF.

———. 1997b. *Republic of Uzbekistan: Recent Economic Developments.* Staff Country Report 97/98. Washington, D.C.: IMF.

———. 2000a. *Republic of Uzbekistan: Recent Economic Developments.* Staff Country Report 00/36. Washington, D.C.: IMF.

———. 2000b. *World Economic Outlook.* Washington, D.C.: IMF.

———. 2002. *Republic of Kazakhstan: Selected Issues and Statistical Appendix.* Country Report 02/64. Washington, D.C.: IMF.

————. 2003a. *Republic of Kazakhstan: Selected Issues and Statistical Appendix.* Country Report 03/211. Washington, D.C.: IMF.

————. 2003b. *Republic of Kazakhstan: 2003 Article IV Consultation—Staff Report.* IMF Country Report 03/210. Washington, D.C.: IMF.

————. 2008a. *Republic of Uzbekistan: Article IV Consultation.* Country Report 08/235. Washington, D.C.: IMF.

————. 2008b. *Republic of Kazakhstan: 2008 Article IV Consultation—Staff Report; Staff Statement and Public Information Notice on Executive Board Discussion.* IMF Country Report No. 08/288. Washington, D.C.: IMF.

Interstate Statistical Committee of the Commonwealth of Independent States (ISCCIS). 2002. *Commonwealth of Independent States in 2001, Statistical Yearbook.* Moscow: ISCCIS.

İpek, Pinar. 2007. The Role of Oil and Gas in Kazakhstan's Foreign Policy: Looking East or West? *Europe-Asia Studies* 59(7): 1179–99.

Isachenkov, Vladimir. 2005. Akayev Signs His Resignation. *Moscow Times,* April 5, p. 3.

Jensen, Camilla. 2006. Foreign Direct Investment and Economic Transition: Panacea or Pain Killer? *Europe-Asia Studies* 58(6): 881–902.

Johnson, Janet, and Richard Joslyn. 1995. *Political Science Research Methods,* 3rd ed. Washington, D.C.: Congressional Quarterly.

Johnston, Daniel. 1994. *International Petroleum Fiscal Systems and Production Sharing Contracts.* Tulsa, Okla.: Penn Well Publishing Co.

Jones Luong, Pauline. 2000. Kazakhstan: The Long Term Costs of Short Term Gains. In *Energy and Conflict in Central Asia and the Caucasus,* ed. Robert Ebel and Rajan Menon. Boulder: Rowman and Littlefield.

————. 2002. *Institutional Change and Political Continuity in Post-Soviet Central Asia: Power, Perception and Pacts.* New York: Cambridge University Press.

————, ed. 2004. *The Transformation of Central Asia: States and Societies from Soviet Rule to Independence.* Ithaca, N.Y.: Cornell University Press.

Jones Luong, Pauline, and Erika Weinthal. 2001. Prelude to the Resource Curse: Explaining Oil and Gas Development Strategies in the Soviet Successor States and Beyond. *Comparative Political Studies* 34(4): 367–99.

————. 2004. Contra Coercion: Russian Tax Reform, Exogenous Shocks and Negotiated Institutional Change. *American Political Science Review* 98(1): 139–52.

Kaiser, Mark J., and Allan G. Pulsipher. 2007. A Review of the Oil and Gas Sector in Kazakhstan. *Energy Policy* 35(2): 1300–1314.

Kandiyoti, Deniz. 2007. Post-Soviet Institutional Design and the Paradoxes of the "Uzbek Path." *Central Asian Survey* 26(1): 31–48.

Karimov, Islam. 1993. *Building the Future: Uzbekistan—Its Own Model for Transition to a Market Economy.* Tashkent: Uzbekistan Publishers.

————. 1998. *Uzbekistan on the Threshold of the Twenty-first Century.* New York: St. Martin's Press.

Karl, Terry Lynn. 1997. *The Paradox of Plenty: Oil Booms and Petro-States.* Berkeley: University of California Press.

————. 2000. Crude Calculations: OPEC Lessons for the Caspian Region. In *Energy and Conflict in Central Asia and the Caucasus,* ed. Robert Ebel and Rajan Menon. Boulder: Rowman and Littlefield.

Kirimli, Meryem. 1997. Uzbekistan in the New World Order. *Central Asian Survey* 16(1): 53–64.

Kornai, János. 1990. *The Road to a Free Economy. Shifting from a Socialist System: The Example of Hungary.* New York: Norton.

Lankes, Hans-Peter, and A. J. Venables. 1996. Foreign Direct Investment in Economic Transition: The Changing Patterns of Investment. *Economics of Transition* 4(2): 331–47.

Lipton, David, and Jeffrey Sachs. 1990. Creating a Market Economy in Eastern Europe: The Case of Poland. *Brookings Papers on Economic Activity* 1:75–133.

Lubin, Nancy. 1984. *Labour and Nationality in Soviet Central Asia.* Princeton, N.J.: Princeton University Press.

Melvin, Neil. 2000. *Transition to Authoritarianism on the Silk Road.* Amsterdam: Harwood Academic Publishers.

Meyer, Klaus. 1998. *Direct Investment in Economies in Transition.* Cheltenham: Edward Elgar.

Meyer, Klaus, and Christina Pind. 1999. The Slow Growth of Foreign Direct Investment in the Soviet Union Successor States. *Economics of Transition* 7(1): 201–14.

Michalet, Charles Albert. 1997. *Strategies of Multinationals and Competition for Foreign Direct Investment: The Opening of Central and Eastern Europe.* Washington, D.C.: World Bank.

Moran, Theodore, ed. 1981. *International Political Risk Assessment: The State of the Art.* Washington, D.C.: School of Foreign Service, Georgetown University.

————. 1998. *Managing International Political Risk: New Tools, Strategies and Techniques for Investors and Financial Institutions.* New York: Blackwell.

————. 1999. *Foreign Direct Investment and Development: The New Policy Agenda for Developing Countries and Economies in Transition.* Washington, D.C.: Institute for International Economics.

————. 2006. *Harnessing Foreign Direct Investment for Development: Policies for Developed and Developing Countries.* Washington, D.C.: Center for Global Development.

Murphy, Jonathan. 2006. Illusory Transition? Elite Reconstitution in Kazakhstan, 1989–2002. *Europe Asia Studies* 58(4): 523–54.

Murrell, Peter. 1992. Evolutionary and Radical Approaches to Economic Reform. *Economics of Planning* 25(1): 79–95.

————, ed. 2001. *Assessing the Value of Law in Transition Economies.* Ann Arbor: University of Michigan Press.

Murrell, Peter, Kathyrn Hendley, Barry Ickes, and Randi Ryterman. 1997. Observations on the use of Law by Russian Enterprises. *Post-Soviet Affairs* 13:19–41.

Murrell, Peter, and Yijiang Wang. 1993. When Privatization Should Be Delayed: The Effects of Communist Legacies on Organizational and Institutional Development. *Journal of Comparative Economics* 17(2): 385–406.

Nazarbayev, Nursultan. 2001. *Epicenter of Peace.* Hollins, N.H.: Puritan Press.

Nolan, Peter. 1995. *China's Rise, Russia's Fall: Politics, Economics and Planning in the Transition from Stalinism.* New York: St. Martin's Press.

Olcott, Martha Brill. 1995. *The Kazakhs.* Stanford, Calif.: Hoover Institution Press.

———. 1997. Democratization and the Growth of Political Participation in Kazakhstan. In *Conflict, Cleavage and Change in Central Asia and the Caucasus,* ed. Karen Dawisha and Bruce Parrott. Cambridge: Cambridge University Press.

———. 1998. The Caspian's False Promise. *Foreign Policy,* Summer, 95–112.

———. 2002. *Kazakhstan: The Unfulfilled Promise.* Washington, D.C.: Carnegie Endowment for International Peace.

———. 2005. *Central Asia's Second Chance.* Washington, D.C.: Carnegie Endowment for International Peace.

Orenstein, Mitchell. 2001. *Out of the Red: Building Capitalism and Democracy in Postcommunist Europe.* Ann Arbor: University of Michigan Press.

Orenstein, Mitchell, and Martine Haas. 2005. Globalization and the Future of the Welfare States in Post-Communist East-Central European Countries. In *Globalization and the Future of the Welfare State,* ed. Miguel Glatzer and Dietrich Rueschemeyer. Pittsburgh: University of Pittsburgh Press.

Organization for Economic Cooperation and Development (OECD). 1996. *Investment Guide for Uzbekistan.* Paris: OECD.

———. 1998. *Investment Guide for Kazakhstan.* Paris: OECD.

Organization for Security and Cooperation in Europe (OSCE). 2006. *Republic of Kazakhstan Presidential Election 4 December 2005: OSCE/ODIHR Election Observation Mission Final Report, 21 February.* Warsaw: OSCE/ODIHR.

———. 2007. *Republic of Uzbekistan Presidential Election 23 December 2007: OSCE/ODIHR Needs Assessment Mission Report, November 28–30.* Warsaw: OSCE/ODIHR.

Perlman, Bruce, and Gregory Gleason. 2007. Cultural Determinism versus Administrative Logic: Asian Values and Administrative Reform in Kazakhstan and Uzbekistan. *International Journal of Public Administration* 30:1327–42.

Pomfret, Richard. 2005. Kazakhstan's Economy since Independence: Does the Oil Boom Offer a Second Chance for Sustainable Development? *Europe-Asia Studies* 57(6): 859–76.

———. 2006. *The Central Asian Economies since Independence.* Princeton, N.J.: Princeton University Press.

Roeder, Philip. 1994. Varieties of Post-Soviet Authoritarian Regimes. *Post-Soviet Affairs* 10(1): 61–101.

Rumer, Boris. 1989. *Soviet Central Asia: "A Tragic Experiment"*. Boston: Unwin Hyman.

———. 1991. Central Asia's Cotton Economy and Its Costs. In *Soviet Central Asia: The Failed Transformation*, ed. William Fierman. Boulder: Westview Press.

———. 1996. Disintegration and Reintegration in Central Asia: Dynamics and Prospects. In *Central Asia in Transition: Dilemmas of Political and Economic Development*, ed. Boris Rumer. New York: M. E. Sharpe.

———. 2005. *Central Asia at the End of the Transition*. New York: M. E. Sharpe.

Russia and Eurasia Documents Annual. 1995. Ed. J. L. Black. Gulf Breeze, Fla.: Academic International Press.

Russia and Eurasia Facts and Figures Annual (REFFA). 1993–96. Ed. Theodore Karasik. Gulf Breeze, Fla.: Academic International Press.

———. 1997–99. Ed. Lawrence Robertson. Gulf Breeze, Fla.: Academic International Press.

———. 2000. Ed. Lawrence Robertson. Gulf Breeze, Fla.: Academic International Press.

Ruziev, Kobil, Dipak Ghosh, and Sheila C. Dow. 2007. The Uzbek Puzzle Revisited: An Analysis of Economic Performance in Uzbekistan since 1991. *Central Asian Survey* 26(1): 7–30.

Schatz, Edward. 2004. *Modern Clan Politics: The Power of "Blood" in Kazakhstan and Beyond*. Seattle: University of Washington Press.

Shiells, Clinton. 2003. FDI and the Investment Climate in the CIS Countries. IMF Policy Discussion Paper PDP/03/05. Washington, D.C.: IMF.

Small, Ian, and Noah Bunce. 2003. The Aral Sea Disaster and the Disaster of International Assistance. *Journal of International Affairs* 56(2): 59–74.

Spechler, Martin. 2007. Authoritarian Politics and Economic Reform in Uzbekistan: Past, Present and Prospects. *Central Asian Survey* 26(2): 185–202.

———. 2008. *The Political Economy of Reform in Central Asia: Uzbekistan under Authoritarianism*. New York: Routledge.

Stephens, Malcolm. 1999. *The Changing Role of Export Credit Agencies*. Washington, D.C.: International Monetary Fund.

Stern, Jonathan. 1995. Oil and Gas in the Former Soviet Union: The Changing Foreign Investment Agenda. In *Investment Opportunities in Russia and the CIS*, ed. David Dyker. Washington, D.C.: Brookings Institution.

———. 2005. *The Future of Russian Gas and Gazprom*. Oxford: Oxford University Press.

Stiglitz, Joseph. 2002. *Globalization and Its Discontents*. New York: Norton.

———. 2007. *Making Globalization Work*. New York: Norton.

Stone, Randall. 2002. *Lending Credibility: The International Monetary Fund and the Post-Communist Transition*. Princeton: Princeton University Press.

Suhir, Elena, and Zlatko Kovach. 2003. Administrative Barriers to Entrepreneurship in

Central Asia. June 30. Center for International Private Enterprise, Washington, D.C.

Svolik, Milan. 2008. Authoritarian Reversals and Democratic Consolidation. *American Political Science Review* 102(2): 153–68.

———. 2009. Power Sharing and Leadership Dynamics in Authoritarian Regimes. *American Journal of Political Science* 53(2): 477–94.

Tsygankov, Andrei. 2001. *Pathways after Empire: National Identity and Foreign Economic Policy in the Post-Soviet World*. Lanham, Md.: Rowman and Littlefield.

United Nations Economic and Social Commission for Asia and the Pacific (UNESCAP). 2006. *Asia-Pacific in Figures*. New York: UNESCAP.

U.S.-Kazakhstan Business Association. 2000. *Kazakhstan: An Investment Prospectus*. Washington, D.C.: U.S.-Kazakhstan Business Association.

Uzbek SSR Tsentral'noe statisticheskoe upravlenie. 1971. *Uzbekistan za gody vos'moi piatileki (1966–1970gg): Kratkii statisticheskii sbornik*. Tashkent: Uzbek SSR.

van Meurs, Anton Pedro Hendrik. 1971. *Petroleum Economics and Offshore Mining Legislation: A Geological Evaluation*. Amsterdam: Elsevier.

Vronskaya, Jeanne, and Vladimir Chuguev. 1992. *The Biographical Dictionary of the Former Soviet Union*. London: Bowker-Saur.

Weinthal, Erika, and Pauline Jones Luong. 2001. Energy Wealth and Tax Reform in Russia and Kazakhstan. *Resources Policy* 27:215–23.

Wendt, Alexander. 1987. The Agent-Structure Problem in International Relations Theory. *International Organization* 41:335–70.

Winiecki, Jan. 1995. The Applicability of Standard Reform Packages to Eastern Europe. *Journal of Comparative Economics* 20(3): 347–67.

Wintrobe, Ronald. 1998. *The Political Economy of Dictatorship*. Cambridge: Cambridge University Press.

Wolf, H. C. 1999. *Transition Strategies: Choices and Outcomes*. Princeton Studies in International Finance, 85. Princeton, N.J.: Princeton University Press.

Wooden, Amanda, and Christoph Stefes. 2009. Multivaried and Interacting Paths of Change in Central Eurasia. In *The Politics of Transition in Central Asia and the Caucasus: Enduring Legacies and Emerging Challenges*, ed. Amanda Wooden and Christoph Stefes. New York: Routledge.

World Bank. 1993a. *Kazakhstan: The Transition to a Market Economy*. Washington, D.C.: World Bank.

———. 1993b. *Uzbekistan: An Agenda for Economic Reform*. Washington, D.C.: World Bank.

———. 1996. *World Development Report 1996: From Plan to Market*. Washington, D.C.: World Bank.

———. 1999. Privatization of the Power and Natural Gas Industries in Hungary and Kazakhstan. World Bank Technical Paper No. 451. Washington, D.C.: World Bank.

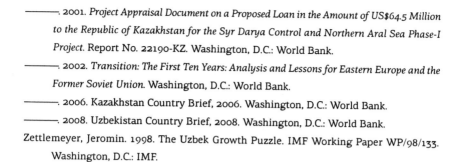

————. 2001. *Project Appraisal Document on a Proposed Loan in the Amount of US$64.5 Million to the Republic of Kazakhstan for the Syr Darya Control and Northern Aral Sea Phase-I Project*. Report No. 22190-KZ. Washington, D.C.: World Bank.

————. 2002. *Transition: The First Ten Years: Analysis and Lessons for Eastern Europe and the Former Soviet Union*. Washington, D.C.: World Bank.

————. 2006. Kazakhstan Country Brief, 2006. Washington, D.C.: World Bank.

————. 2008. Uzbekistan Country Brief, 2008. Washington, D.C.: World Bank.

Zettlemeyer, Jeromin. 1998. The Uzbek Growth Puzzle. IMF Working Paper WP/98/133. Washington, D.C.: IMF.

# Index

**A**

Afghanistan, 8, 32, 86

agriculture: business in, 73; in Uzbekistan, 21, 23; minister of, in Uzbekistan, 39, 87; minister of, in Kazakhstan, 52. *See also* Virgin Lands Campaign

Aral Sea, 22

Article VIII obligations, 41–43, 61, 90

Asanbayev, Yerik, 51–52

Åslund, Anders, 3–6, 11, 93

authoritarianism, 3, 10, 41, 70, 87, 97

**B**

Balgimbayev, Nurlan, 62

Brezhnev, Leonid, 15, 24–26

Business Environment and Enterprise Performance Surveys (BEEPS), 71

**C**

Caspian Sea, 17

Central Eastern European and Baltic States reform policies, 2–4, 11, 94

clans: in Kazakhstan, 10; in Uzbekistan, 31

coal production, 16–17, 95

Cotton Affair, 25–26, 31, 95

cotton, 2, 8, 12, 15, 20–26, 29, 31, 35–42, 45, 73, 95–96

Cummings, Sally, 8, 52–53

currency convertibility, 4, 42, 87 ; in Kazakhstan, 2, 7, 44, 63, 88; in Uzbekistan, 2, 41–43, 45, 63, 89–91; risks mitigated by US Export Import Bank, 87, 91. *See also* economic reform

**D**

Dzhurabekov, Ismail, 31, 33–34, 38–39

**E**

economic reform, 1–9, 11–12, 15, 67, 97, 99; Central and Eastern Europe and the Baltic States, 2–3; divergent processes of, in Kazakhstan and Uzbekistan, 1, 2, 11–12, 27, 59, 62, 67,

72; IMF economists on, 2, 6, 12, 40, 42; importance of, for investment and business decisions, 72–78, 80, 83–84, 88, 91, 99; in Kazakhstan, 1, 2, 10, 13, 15, 47, 50–52, 54, 59, 63, 65, 67, 72, 88, 93, 98; in Uzbekistan, 1, 2, 6, 8–10, 12, 19, 27, 33, 35–36, 38, 40, 42, 44–45, 67, 72, 88, 93, 98; natural resources, role in, 72–73, 75–77, 80, 91, 99; strategies of, 4–6, 31, 94, 99; U.S. Export-Import Bank role in, 83–84, 88. *See also* Karimov, Islam, economic reform policies of; Nazarbayev, Nursultan, economic reform policies of
electrical production, 7, 16, 95
European Bank for Reconstruction and Development (EBRD): 12, 34–35, 38, 43–44, 51–52, 60, 63, 68–73, 79, 81–83, 88–89, 94; transition ratings of, 43–44, 63, 89; and FDI amounts, 12, 68–69
Export Credit Agency, 67, 83–88, 91, 99
Extended Fund Facility (EFF), 59–60

**F**
financial crisis (2008): effects of, in Kazakhstan, 64–65, 99; effects of, in Uzbekistan, 44–45, 64, 98, 99
Fischer, Stanley, 4, 11, 59, 68
foreign exchange: 32, 35–36, 38, 42, 45, 70–71, 85, 90, 96; system of, 11, 34, 42–44, 63, 90

**G**
Gazprom, 19
Gleason, Gregory, 11, 98
gold, 8, 20, 35–38, 41, 45, 68, 73–74, 95

Gorbachev, Mikhail, 26, 30–31, 48
gradualists as an approach to economic reform, 5, 6, 94, 98–99

**H**
Hellman, Joel, 9, 11, 32, 96

**I**
International Monetary Fund (IMF) ,1; Kazakhstan and, 2, 10, 55, 59, 65, 81; Uzbekistan and, 2, 37, 35, 40–42, 59, 89–90
investment: 6, 7, 11–13, 18, 65, 67–81, 86, 91, 97, 99: in Kazakhstan, 16, 51–52, 60, 68, 73, 75–76, 82, 92; in Uzbekistan, 18–20, 34, 36, 38, 45, 69, 73, 75–77, 82–83, 87, 92. *See also* economic reform, importance of, for investment and business decisions
Islamic Movement of Uzbekistan, 32

**J**
Jones Luong, Pauline, 7, 72, 82

**K**
Karimov, Islam, 29–33, 39, 47; continuation of Sharif Rashidov policies by, 26, 29, 31; and Cotton Affair, 26, 31; coup attempt in Moscow, 30; economic reform policies of, 29, 31–33, 38, 49, 61–62, 95, 99–100; as first secretary of Communist Party of Uzbek SSR, 3, 26; government of, 18, 40, 45, 57, 77, 87, 95; policies of, on cotton production, 15, 38–39; and presidential elections, 3, 30–31, 43, 44; and Soviet-era elite, 9–10, 29–33, 35, 38, 40, 47, 49–51, 61, 96–97, 100;

public record of, 13, 27, 31–32

Kazakhstan: constitution of, 58–59; economic reform of, 1–7, 10, 12–13, 27, 42–43, 47, 49, 51, 60–61, 63, 72, 88, 93, 98; elite in, 10–12, 33; irrigation systems in, 22; legislation in, 79–81, 83, 88; natural resource sector and, 16–18, 23, 52, 60, 64, 68–69, 70–71; and nuclear weapons, 49–50; People's Assembly of, 57; population in, 24; integration of, with Russia, 7–8, 12, 15–18, 23–24, 63–64, 72, 93, 95; U.S. Embassy of, 106n8. *See also* Nazarbayev, Nursultan

Kazhegeldin, Akezhan, 56–57, 61–62

Khamidov, Bakhtyar, 34, 38–40

Khrushchev, Nikita, 21

Kunayev, Dinmukhamed, 24, 26, 48–49, 96

**L**

LUKoil, 19

**M**

Massimov, Karim, 62, 65

Mirsaidov, Shakarulla, 30–33

Moran, Theodore, 70, 81

Multiple Exchange Rate Regime, 2, 13, 29, 37–38, 41, 43–44

**N**

National Fund of the Republic of Kazakhstan (NFRK), 64

natural gas sector: in Kazakhstan, 60, 64, 68, 71, 74; in Uzbekistan, 8, 18–20, 45, 68, 74, 76, 95

natural resource sector, 68, 70–71, 76, 98–99

Nazarbayev, Nursultan, 29, 47–49; and attracting investment, 79, 80–81, 87; and Dinmukhamed Kunayev, 26, 48–49, 96; economic reform policies of, 10, 13, 47, 49–53, 56–58, 61–65, 93, 95, 99–100; as first secretary of the Communist Party of Kazakh SSR, 3, 26; government of, 10, 18, 29, 50–52, 56–57, 59, 61–62, 65, 95, 97–98; and Kazakh Constitutional Court, 57–58, 96; and Mikhail Gorbachev, 48; and new constitution of Kazakhstan, 47, 57–59; and new elite in Kazakhstan, 9, 50, 56, 61–62, 96–97; on nuclear weapons, 49, 50; and parliaments, 10, 13, 47, 52–59, 62–63, 80, 96, 98; and presidential elections, 3, 57, 62–63; and rule by presidential decree, 10, 13, 47, 58–59, 96; public record of, 27, 48–50, 56–58, 62, 64, 65, 81; Soviet-era elite, 9–10, 47–51, 53, 56, 93, 96, 100; and United States, 50

**O**

oil sector: foreign investment in, 68, 70–71, 73–74, 76, 80–81; in Kazakhstan, 7, 16–18, 63–64, 73, 80–81, 95; in Uzbekistan, 35, 73, 83; lack of pipeline for, 7, 16–18, 71, 95; and resource curse, 64, 72

Olcott, Martha Brill, 9, 10, 16, 24, 48, 52, 57, 61, 63

Organization for Security and Cooperation in Europe (OSCE), 44, 63, 96

**P**

Parliament: in Kazakhstan, 10, 13, 47, 50–63, 80, 96; in Uzbekistan, 9–10, 96

Pomfret, Richard, 6, 70, 98

poverty: in Uzbekistan, 45; in Kazakhstan, 63

prime ministers: in Kazakhstan, 51–52, 54–56, 58–59, 62, 65; in Uzbekistan, 32–34, 39–40, 77

**R**

Rashidov, Sharif, 25–26, 29–31, 33, 39, 95

rent-seeking, 5, 72

rents, 9, 45, 73, 96–97

Representatives: of U.S. firms,13, 67, 71–74, 91, 97; business, 74, 77, 84–88, 90–91, 97, 99; natural resource, 74–77, 80, 91, 97, 99; service, 74, 77–78, 91, 97

risk, 69, 71, 75, 82, 84, 91; alleviated by U.S. Export Import Bank, 84–87, 91, 99; of conducting business, 67, 69, 71, 84, 86–87, 89, 99; of investment, 69–70, 76–78, 91; of services, 78

Rumer, Boris, 6, 21–22, 24, 25, 98

**S**

Shkolnik, Vladimir, 57, 59

shock therapy as approach to economic reform, 4, 6, 31, 99

*Soum (sum)*, 34, 82

Stand-by Arrangement (SBA), 35, 37, 43, 55, 59

Svolik, Milan, 97–98

**T**

tenge, 52, 64

**U**

U.S. Export-Import Bank, 67, 83–88, 91, 99

Uzbekistan: constitution of, 32; demographics of, 22–23, 87; economic reform in, 1–7, 9, 12–13, 19, 27, 35–36, 42–43, 72–73, 88, 90, 93, 96, 97–99; elite in, 9–10, 26, 33, 97; embassy, 31, 40, 73, 82; government in, 8–9, 25–26, 30, 32, 38, 45, 57, 86–87; irrigation systems in, 22; legislation in, 65, 67, 82–83, 99; natural resource sector and, 8, 18–20, 68, 76, 82, 99; presidential elections in, 3, 43; and Russia, 8, 12, 15, 18–19, 23–24, 93, 95. *See also* Islam Karimov

**V**

Virgin Lands Campaign, 21, 23–24

**W**

World Bank, 4–5, 10, 22, 37, 45, 62–63, 71, 94; Kazakhstan and, 7, 16–18, 22, 60, 61, 64; Uzbekistan and, 20–23, 45

**Z**

Zettlemeyer, Jeromin, 19, 93